Pilgrims
not Strangers

Pilgrims

not Strangers

Christian Witness
in a Broken World

by Carlo Maria Martini
Archbishop of Milan

Translated by
Mary James Berger, fsp

St. Paul Books & Media

Library of Congress Cataloging-in-Publication Data

Martini, Carlo M.
     [Cammini laicali. English]
          Pilgrims, not strangers: Christian witness in a broken world /
by Carlo Maria Martini; translated by Mary James Berger.
     p.   cm.
     ISBN 0-8198-5888-9
     1. Meditations.   I. Title
BX2185.M33713   1993
242--dc20 93-6448
CIP

Original title: *Cammini laicali.*

Translated from the Italian by Mary James Berger, fsp

Printed and published in the U.S.A. by St. Paul Books & Media
50 St. Paul's Avenue, Boston, MA 02130

St. Paul Books & Media is the publishing house of the Daughters of
St. Paul, an international congregation of women religious serving the Church
with the communications media.

1   2   3   4   5   6   7   8   9   99   98   97   96   95   94   93

Contents

II. Troubled Families in the Bible

Presentation

"For in Christ Jesus you are all children of God through faith. As many of you as were *baptized* into Christ have clothed yourselves with Christ" (Gal 3:26-27). And again St. Paul writes: "We know that all things work together for good for those who love God, who are called according to his purpose. For those whom he foreknew he also predestined to be *conformed* to the image of his Son" (Rom 8:28-29).

The Apostle thus describes the two conditions of the Christian life: the first is that of Baptism, which causes us to *be in Christ*; the second condition unfolds from the first throughout the span of the person's existence, namely, the condition of mature faith, of *full configuration with Christ*. It is the call to live as children of God, as brothers and sisters of the only Son of the Father.

In this common vocation to become sons and daughters, the infinite mystery of God revealed in the crucified and risen Jesus is made present in the Church through the different states in life: the lay, the clerical, and the religious. Each of these forms of following Christ has its own original and unmistakable features, yet they complete one another and form a unity.

The Second Vatican Council, which has marvelously re-expressed in new ways the various functions or missions of the members of the People of God, also had the merit of bringing us to understand the profile of the *Christian laity*. In fact the laity's mission is not only the Christian animation of temporal realities; it involves a specific response to Jesus' mandate to announce the Kingdom.

And within the lay state, the rich variety of the Church finds a further manifestation of vocations or paths.

Pilgrims Not Strangers recalls two: the matrimonial vocation and that of secular institutes. The matrimonial vocation is fundamental insofar as it is a sign of every call to "be together," therefore a sign of the Church, a sign of humanity, a sign of all the men and women on earth called to form one Body in Christ. The vocation to secular institutes is proper to those persons who profess the evangelical counsels of poverty, chastity and obedience, so as to tend to the perfection of charity, living in the world and dealing directly with daily realities, committing themselves for the sanctification of history.

This small volume contains the meditations which Carlo Maria Cardinal Martini, Archbishop of Milan, gave on the occasion of two brief spiritual retreats. The first was given to the members of a secular institute (the Institute of the Missionaries of the Kingship of Christ, which began in 1928 and was canonically erected in 1951); the second to families which belong to a movement promoting matrimonial spirituality (the *Equipe Notre Dame*, which began in Paris in 1939 and has spread through Italy since 1959).

The meditations and points for contemplation offered by this book will be a stimulus to all those who, whether in family life or the life of consecration, seek to discover God's plan of salvation in every event and in every situation, and who, by giving their lives for their brothers and sisters, seek to manifest with joy the face of Jesus Son of the Father, knowing that each one is called to live "like good stewards of the manifold grace of God, (serving) one another with whatever gift each of you has received" (1 Pet 4:10).

Part One
Being with Jesus

❖   ❖   ❖

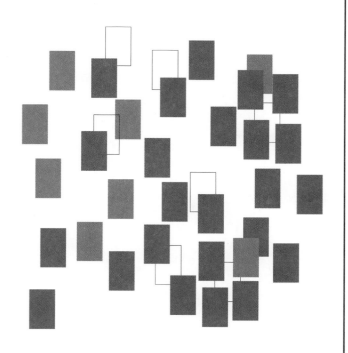

Dying to Sin

Premise

This is the first time, in recent years, that I have been able to spend some moments in prolonged prayer with the members of a secular institute.

Therefore our encounter is also symbolic, for I intend to place myself in harmony and in a communion of faith with all the secular institutes in the Church, with a desire to grasp the gift of God present in so many realities similar to yours.

I thought to offer you some points for meditation on a theme suggested to me by the feast of Mary's assumption into heaven, which almost certainly took place in Jerusalem in the year 51. In preparing the homily for the Pontifical Mass which is celebrated every year in the Cathedral on August 15, I contemplated Mary as the first *believer*, and therefore as the model of our earthly pilgrimage, a figure of the Church, who is now definitively with Jesus.

Thus the title for Part One of our reflections: "Being with Jesus, together with Mary assumed into heaven." The dogma of the Assumption was proclaimed in 1950, as you recall, and it seems to me important to keep in mind this event which is so significant for the history of the Church in the twentieth century. The theological debate about the assumption of Mary, in fact, influenced the whole faith atmosphere of the immediate post-war period and accompanied, in a manner of speaking, the years of Italy's reconstruction. However, after the definition of the dogma, reflection has lessened somewhat, perhaps because attention was directed first to the announcement and then to the development of the Second Vatican Council.

In a conference given in May of 1948, during the Fourth Spirituality Week of the Catholic University, Father Agostino Gemelli spoke of "Mary most holy as model and guide of the spiritual life."

We want to contemplate her in this light, as a model and guide for living with Jesus until the fulfillment of our earthly pilgrimage.

In your personal meditation I suggest that you reread some of the texts of the Church's magisterium: the Bull of the dogmatic definition of 1950; the Constitution *Lumen Gentium* of Vatican II (nn. 62-69); *Marialis Cultus* by Pope Paul VI, dated February 2, 1974 (n. 27); and finally *Redemptoris Mater* by John Paul II (nn. 5-6).

* I will refer first of all to biblical sources, especially to some passages of the New Testament. While they do not all speak explicitly of Mary, they contain an understanding of the Christian mystery that will enlighten us on our journey. They are drawn from the Gospel of Mark and the Letters of Paul.

* I will also cite some texts concerning the life of St. Francis of Assisi and some from the *Autobiography* of Ignatius of Loyola, because his conversion is in a certain sense linked with the vocation of Francis. Ignatius recounts that two books were determining factors in his decision to radically change his way of life: a *Life of Christ* (therefore the meditation of the mysteries along the Franciscan line) and a *Life of the Saints*. "In reading the life of our Lord and of the saints, he began" (Ignatius speaks of himself in the third person) "to think and to reflect: 'And if I too were to do what St. Francis and St. Dominic have done?'...

"His whole reasoning was a repetition: St. Dominic did this, I too must do it; St. Francis did this, I too must do it" (*Autobiography*, n. 7).

St. Francis was one of his models, and some typical actions of Ignatius recall those of the "poverello" of Assisi.

* Finally I want to take into account the Constitutions of your Institute, the Missionaries of the Kingship of Christ, in the form which I approved on June 13, 1980, and then on September 18, 1989; especially n. 5: "Our teacher, model and strength is the incarnate Word of God, in whom human and divine realities are joined. In his history we find the meaning of our own." "Living with Jesus" not only in the abstract, but in his history: "from the humblest beginnings in Bethlehem to the exile in Egypt, from the simple and laborious life of Nazareth to the apostolate in Galilee, in Judea, in pagan territory; from the paschal supper to the cross, death and resurrection."

This first meditation will include three points:

* the desire to be with Jesus;

* the baptismal dynamism of being with Jesus;

* the first stage of being with Jesus.

We now begin by recollecting ourselves in silence and prayer:

"God our Father, we thank you for the gifts you have given to Mary most holy, the Mother of your Son, whom you have called to be with him in the fullness of glory. We ask that you enable us to understand the heart of Mary, the heart of Christ your Son and the dynamism of the baptismal life by which we are made sharers in the journey of Christ, of Mary and of your saints. Grant that by contemplating this journey,

we may feel consoled in our daily struggles, reassured amid the uncertainties of our journey, full of enthusiasm in moments of fatigue. You see how we strive to keep our gaze fixed on heaven while the horizon seems restricted to the earth. Let the heavens be opened and permit us to intuit what we are journeying toward, to be with Mary and with Jesus who lives and reigns with you in the unity of the Holy Spirit, for ever and ever. Amen."

The Desire to Be with Jesus

1. We begin with a passage from the Letter to the Philippians. Paul is in prison, in a situation of absolute uncertainty. While thinking of what might await him in the future he writes: "For to me, living is Christ and dying is gain. If I am to live in the flesh, that means fruitful labor for me; and I do not know which I prefer. I am hard pressed between the two: my desire is to depart and be with Christ, for that is far better; but to remain in the flesh is more necessary for you" (Phil 1: 21-24).

Let us reflect on these words: "my desire is to depart and be with Christ." The term "desire" in the original Greek is *epithymìa*, which means "a craving," especially for corporal goods, and which is often used in the Bible in a negative sense (lust, concupiscence, uncontrollable burning passion). Paul applies it to being with Christ to indicate that his desire is not purely intellectual but possesses his body, his life, his affections. In this positive sense the term *epithymìa* is used by Jesus in the Gospel of Luke: "I have eagerly desired to eat this Passover with you" (Lk 22:15). And again from Paul in the First Letter to the Thessalonians: "When, for a short time, we were made orphans by being separated from you—in person, not in heart—we longed with great eagerness to see you face to face" (1 Thess 2:17). It is the ardent desire of one who loves and wants to communicate with the beloved, wants to see him or her face to face. In view of Paul's expression in the Letter to the Philippians, we can think that if the Apostle desired so strongly to "see" Jesus whom he had never seen on earth, how much more Mary must have desired it. We are invited to contemplate Our Lady, all afire with the longing to see her Son again, to be seated at the table in the fullness of the heavenly banquet, even with her whole corporeal being, for this forms part of the mystery of the redemption: a redemption of soul and body, the glorification of the whole human person.

To be with Jesus is thus the longing of Paul and the longing of Mary.

2. But it is also the longing of Francis: "Welcome to my sister bodily death." And when he is close to death: "The saint raised his hands to heaven, glorifying his Christ, because he was able to go freely to him, without hindrance of any sort." This desire is linked to poverty: Francis is free and, with total joy, wants to go to his Lord. A desire and joy that manifest themselves not so much in total detachment from earthly things as in freedom and the taste for common things: "While the brothers were shedding bitter tears and complaining in desolation, the saint instead was full of joy and had such liberty of spirit as to ask for some parsley or to show a desire to taste for the last time certain sweets of Brother James." And then Francis says to his brothers: "I hasten toward God and entrust you all to his grace" (cf *Dizionario Francescano*, Padua: Messaggero, 1983, 1055-1063).

3. In his *Autobiography*, Ignatius of Loyola speaks several times of the desire for death, which permitted him to face the most dangerous voyages without any fear and to accept illness with serenity. This expression is especially interesting: "In 1550 he was very ill due to a serious sickness which, in his judgment and that of others, seemed to be his last. On this occasion the thought of death brought him such joy and he was so spiritually

consoled at having to die that he melted into tears. This emotion became so habitual to him that he often had to stop thinking about death so as not to feel such intense consolation" (*Autobiography*, n. 33).

I invite you to reflect on the experience of Francis and Ignatius—which is evidently the fruit of very special graces—and compare it with ours. It is true that we can say: all this is too far removed from us. We will perhaps never desire death as ardently as that. However, we must recognize that no Christian can avoid questioning himself on this point. Not only is the desire for eternal life in keeping with baptismal life, but it is its constitutive and essential aspect.

The Baptismal Dynamism of Being with Jesus

1. To be with Jesus is thus the focal point of our life of faith, which is rooted in *baptismal dynamism*.

Romans 6:4-5, 8: "Therefore we have been buried with him by baptism into death, so that, just as Christ was raised from the dead by the glory of the Father, so too, we might walk in newness of life. For if we have been united with him in a death like his, we will certainly be united with him in a resurrection like his." Completely united with him, made one with him in death. Our "being with Jesus" begins by being "buried with him into death." And in verse 8: "But if we have died *with* Christ, we believe that we will also live *with* him."

Baptism places us with Jesus, not in a static companionship but on a journey that goes from death and the grave unto the fullness of being with Jesus in glory, like Mary.

Karl Rahner writes that baptismal dynamism is the essence of Christian eschatology. The eschatological affirmations of the New Testament—death, judgment, hell, heaven—are the necessary consequences in view of human nature, deriving from the experience of the

Christian *present*. We project this present into the future because man cannot understand his own present except as the springing up, the becoming, the dynamic toward a reality "beyond."

We must understand the individual actions of our lives in this perspective. Each time we reduce life to a present not open to the future, we lock it into sadness, banality, distrust. This is the great drama of the contemporary world which, shutting itself off from eternal realities, seeks to satisfy itself with present, earthly ideals which may be good but which impede the fullness of hope. This inevitably leads to a frustration of activity or to self-destruction. When we do not succeed in accomplishing what we hoped and have no other horizons, we feel defeated and act out these feelings in a dramatic way, reaching extreme consequences. Therefore humanity is profoundly wounded and mutilated by the lack of that perspective which, instead, Christians live as something inherent in their baptismal dynamism.

2. To be with the Lord, however, is not only the expression of baptismal dynamism, but is also the "Christian" expression of the *universal dynamism of love*.

All of history is moved by love, which is a constructive force; it is the tendency toward the good. But the highest good is the personal good; therefore love tends toward the fullest and most definitive communion with the most personal and absolute good: God. The movement toward the union of humanity with God is the immanent law of history; a law that is expressed, on the level of faith, in Baptism, and yet is also a physical and psychological law that governs the movement of the world.

3. To be with Jesus is, in addition, the *fundamental dynamism of the apostolic life*.

Mark 3:14: Jesus "went up the mountain and called to him those whom he wanted, and they came to him.

And he appointed twelve, whom he also named apostles, *to be with him.*" The expression is much stronger in the Greek: *"that they might be with him."*

Whoever is involved in the apostolate has this "being with Jesus" as a reference point. The rest follows: "and to be sent out to proclaim the message, and to have authority to cast out demons." First of all we must "be," we must "stay" with Jesus.

In conclusion we can say that our life has meaning to the degree that *we stay with Jesus,* Son of the Father, letting ourselves be conquered and attracted by his love in order to be conformed to him in all things.

The First Stage of Being with Jesus

This staying, this being with Jesus has a history, has stages, expresses itself as a journey.

To understand the various stages we will again look at the text of the Letter to the Romans, in which Paul presents a stupendous synthesis, rich in pathos, of the baptismal event. He is able to express it because he has experienced in his life what in reality Christ has done for him.

The first stage is *dying to sin with Jesus*: "Do you not know that all of us who have been baptized into Christ Jesus were baptized into his *death?*" Immediately afterwards he emphasizes the consequences of this baptism into death: *buried* with Jesus, *completely united* with him, *our old self has been crucified* with him (cf Rom 6:4-6). And again: "Therefore do not let sin *exercise dominion* in your mortal bodies, to make you obey their passions. *No longer present* your members to sin as instruments of wickedness, but present yourselves to God as those who have been brought from death to life, and present your members to God as instruments of righteousness. For sin will have no dominion over you" (Rom 6:12-14).

We can interpret the words of the Apostle by saying

that, thanks to the baptismal transformation which has united us to the death and burial of Jesus, and thanks to the baptismal strength which fights in us the battle against sin, we "have done" with the dominion of sin.

1. To die to sin, in fact, implies a *fundamental option*, which follows upon baptismal grace and which is to be kept alive: the option not to fall into serious sin, which separates us from Jesus.

In his *Spiritual Exercises*, St. Ignatius expresses this decision in the so-called *first form of humility:* "Even if I were to be made master of all the created things of this world, or at the cost of my own physical life, I would not dare to decide to break any commandment, divine or human, that binds me under pain of mortal sin" (n. 165).

It is a gift that we must always ask for in prayer, because it includes martyrdom, it puts our life at risk. As a consequence of their Baptism each baptized person is called to enter into this absolute and fundamental decision.

Those who study moral theology ask themselves whether such an option is compatible with seriously sinful acts, that is, whether of its nature it exonerates us definitively from the danger of sin.

Experience warns us that even where there is a firm, decided will, the risk of falling is never absent, because the human person is a reality in process, a complex, confused reality, composed of many levels. The decision does not immediately and totally reach all the levels, and a whole lifetime is needed for it to attain complete dominion in us.

However, even if sin does surprise us, we succeed in recognizing and confessing it. In those, instead, who have not made this firm decision, a sin only serves to deepen the decadence of the preceding sin.

The fundamental option is therefore a very important grace. It stems from having understood, in the contemplation of the crucified Christ, that his death has snatched me from slavery to sin, that Jesus has died for me and in Baptism has given me his salvation event. But this grace does not reach us once for all and therefore must always be rebuilt, extended, and increased, through prayer and the cultivation of the spiritual life, knowing that the fundamental option is an antidote against sin and has value as a force for beginning again, for a courageous renewal.

2. The second step of "dying to sin" is accomplished in *dying to what is advantageous to self,* so as to enter always more deeply into that attitude of Jesus which led him not to do his own will but the will of the One who sent him. We must seek to live above all the first part of this attitude. "I can do nothing on my own. As I hear, I judge; and my judgment is just, because *I seek to do not my own will...*" (Jn 5:30).

Not seeking one's own will is equivalent to living *interior freedom,* which St. Ignatius of Loyola calls the *second form of humility,* more perfect than the first. We live it when we find ourselves in the "condition of not wanting and not even feeling inclined to possess riches rather than poverty, honor rather than dishonor, or to desire a long rather than a short life" (*Spiritual Exercises,* n. 166). It is the invitation not to seek one's own advantage in anything, to have a sovereign freedom of heart. He continues: "On the basis of this, one does not dare decide to commit a venial sin, even if it were in exchange for all of creation or at the cost of one's life." It is interesting to consider the relationship between interior freedom, which does not incline either to riches or to poverty, to honor or dishonor, to a long life or a short one, and the decision not to commit any venial sin.

This attitude is still not the choice of poverty, which as we will see forms part of the life of the Risen One; however, it is its premise, it is a state of interior availability. "I mean, brothers and sisters, the appointed time has grown short; from now on, let even those who have wives be as though they had none, and those who mourn as though they were not mourning, and those who rejoice as though they were not rejoicing, and those who buy as though they had no possessions, and those who deal with the world as though they had no dealings with it. For the present form of this world is passing away" (1 Cor 7:29-31). Looking to Jesus as the definitive goal changes the perspective of time and, for the baptized person, makes all things relative. Even before a positive evangelical choice (for example, poverty), there is already that freedom, that readiness, that detachment of one who is in the presence of the absolute of the Lord and of the certainty of eternal life already possessed. Such a state of freedom expresses the baptismal renunciation, the condition of having died with Christ, and it is the root of every just Christian choice. There is no true choice without this interior availability.

I would like, finally, to recall the many names which Francis of Assisi gave to sin, because they show how firm was his decision to "be with Jesus," to be dead to sin. He speaks of "crime, blindness, falsity, apostasy, ugliness, deceit, misery, baseness, decay, ingratitude, malice." We know that his baptismal option was so strong as to enable him to resist the greatest temptations.

And the radicalness of his vocational choice can be considered as the expression of that freedom of heart which marked both the attitude and behavior of Francis with regard to everything and everyone: persons, things, power in any form.

I therefore invite you to contemplate the pierced heart of Christ, in a spirit of humility, because the first degree of our "being with Jesus" needs to be continually verified within us. We are, in fact, weak and fragile, and we live in an environment which does not help us hold to our fundamental decision, to struggle against that sin which is seriously harmful to the development of human existence because it engulfs that existence and ruins it interiorly, morally and physically.

The Jerusalem
Which Descends from on High

(Homily for the Mass of St. Bartholomew Apostle)

The Goal of the Earthly Pilgrimage

In the plan of God, the goal of the pilgrimage of human life is expressed with different names, each of which indicates a different aspect.

Thus we speak, for example, of "eternal life," meaning the fullness of life without end, the life already begun in Baptism.

Or we speak of the "beatific vision," in reference to the individual aspect of reaching the end of our pilgrimage, with the connotation, however, that even now—even if darkly as through a mirror, as through an enigma—we can contemplate and enjoy this mystery.

We also speak of "kingdom," that is, the fullness and totality of the goal, when we will live with him who is the head, the Lord, Jesus Christ.

And "heaven" alludes to the horizon of the whole human journey, to the horizon which is also the end of the ascending journey of the human person, to the overcoming of self to the point of identification with him who draws us from on high, the Father in the Son.

We speak also of the "heavenly Jerusalem," to emphasize the social, collective aspect of this fullness.

In the readings of today's liturgy we find some references to this final end which marks the point of arrival of our pilgrimage.

Mary and the Heavenly Jerusalem

"Then one of the seven angels...came and said to me, 'Come, I will show you the bride, the wife of the Lamb.' And in the spirit he carried me away to a great, high mountain and showed me the holy city Jerusalem coming down out of heaven from God. It has the glory of God and a radiance like a very rare jewel, like jasper, clear as crystal. It has a great, high wall with twelve gates, and at the gates twelve angels, and on the gates are inscribed the names of the twelve tribes of the Israelites; on the east three gates, on the north three gates, on the south three gates, and on the west three gates. And the wall of the city has twelve foundations, and on them are the twelve names of the twelve apostles of the Lamb" (Rev 21:9-14).

Jerusalem, of which the visionary of the Book of Revelation speaks, marks the end of the human journey, with reference to the holy city, the goal of Israel's pilgrimages and of Jesus' pilgrimage beginning from his twelfth year. The whole life of Jesus is described, especially by the evangelist Luke, as a pilgrimage toward Jerusalem. For this reason it recalls to the Christian the baptismal commitment to be with Jesus, in his death, in his burial and then in his resurrection.

Jerusalem points to a whole people's "being with the Lord," in such a way as to construct a new, holy city, which stands in opposition to the first city built by Cain (cf Gen 4:17). The city of Cain, constructed as a remedy for his own incurable solitude, is characterized by a lack of fraternity and would soon become the city of Babel, confused and incapable of a common project (cf Gen 11:1-9). The holy city Jerusalem thus redeems ancient Babel and expresses the journey of a humanity which cultivates fraternity, togetherness, solidarity, a common plan to be carried out with and in God.

In the Psalms the word "Jerusalem" is a symbol of our desire to see God, to see him in the heavens, in eternal fullness.

However, in the passage cited from Revelation (cf Rev 21:9-14) Jerusalem is contemplated in an unusual manner, as a city "descending from on high," resplendent with the glory of God.

Why is it, as compared to the ordinary image in which Jerusalem is the end of the journey, that here it descends toward humankind?

I believe that, inasmuch as it is the end of the journey, it emphasizes the goal which humanity struggles to reach; as the city descending from on high, instead, it is the final image of this fullness which progressively occupies human reality. While on the one hand history is a fatiguing ascent, on the other it is the realization of Jerusalem which comes from heaven to take possession of it.

We speak of that positive vision to which we have already alluded: the truth of history is a gift which descends from on high, from God, and fills humankind with divine glory.

Jerusalem is the city which is gradually realized in time; it is the communion of the saints which, beginning with Mary and the holy people of the Old Testament, with the apostles and then all the people who reach the fullness of life with the Lord, is being formed in the world. There is, therefore, a heavenly multitude which fills history, invades it, even if apparently it is unseen, even if its presence is veiled, hidden.

With the eyes of faith, however, we can contemplate it because it is, in part, accomplished. It is accomplished, in the final moment, in Mary who is the image of redeemed humanity and who enfolds us with her "radiance like a very rare jewel, like jasper, clear as crystal." This reality is well defined in itself, "a great, high wall with *twelve* gates," open to all four cardinal points. Though a singular figure, Mary is accessible to all humanity, can be understood by all, and all can enter into her, from every part of the earth. As a reference she has the number *twelve:* twelve is the number of fullness, and it is also the number of the twelve tribes of Israel, because Mary is the synthesis of all humankind.

However, the Jerusalem coming down from heaven as the spouse of the Lamb, which finds in Mary its perfect image, is realized even now on earth. Here, to the eyes of faith, the Church is radiant as a very rare jewel, it is the spouse of the Lamb. It is well distinguished by a great, high wall which, however, has twelve gates; it is open to all peoples. "The wall of the city has twelve foundations, and on them are the names of the twelve apostles of the Lamb." This Church is founded on the Twelve and their successors; thus, even its institutional character comes from God and penetrates history.

The passage from Revelation, rich in symbolism, is open to very broad applications, and can be read on various levels, once we have the global vision of the divine mystery.

The Mystery of God in History

And what is promised to us? The promise received by Nathaniel, by the apostle Bartholomew when he asked Jesus: "Where did you get to know me?" Jesus answered: "Do you believe because I told you that I saw you under the fig tree? You will see greater things than these!" Then he said: "Very truly, I tell you, you will see the heavens opened and the angels of God ascending and descending upon the Son of Man" (Jn 1:48-51).

If you are faithful to grace, you will see the heavens opened, you will understand ever better the mystery of God in human history, you will grasp how that mystery is Jesus who unites heaven and earth, who allows the heavenly Jerusalem to occupy history; it is our being with Jesus.

When he wrote the Book of Revelation, John was experiencing difficult moments under the pressure of persecution, humiliation and suffering. His words and visions express that openness of perspective which is possible to us every time we walk with Christ in poverty and humiliation. Then we see the heavens opened and we contemplate the truth of history.

We have great need of this contemplation because often the Church, in its historical journey, is lacking in consolations; it grieves, becomes disheartened, becomes dejected, blames itself, perhaps excessively, feels unequal to its mission, has the impression of being abandoned by its Lord. It is therefore necessary to comfort the Church through these visions of faith which allow it to perceive, even along its path of tribulations, the Jerusalem coming down from on high, of which the Church itself is already the beginning.

Each one of you can be a witness to such a faith, in a Church tempted by fatigue, by shortsightedness—not seeing the heavens opened.

Each one of you is called to witness to this faith and this hope, present in St. Bartholomew and in all the apostles, after the example of Mary.

Let us ask the Lord for the grace to contemplate in the Eucharist the Jerusalem which comes down from heaven, because the Eucharist is already the heavenly life realized in time. Let us ask to contemplate it in order to let the dew of God's consolation permeate our life, to express our faith with joy and happiness in our daily living.

Being with the Risen Jesus

Having reflected on the first stage of being with Jesus (that is, being dead with him through Baptism), we now want to consider the more constructive aspect of the profile of the Christian, that is, being with the risen Jesus.

We will reflect on some biblical texts according to the method of the *lectio divina*.

Lectio of Romans 6 and Colossians 3

* Romans 6:4b, 5b, 8, 11. Let us reread the verses of the Letter to the Romans, emphasizing, however, the words which refer to the Resurrection: "Just as Christ was *raised* from the dead by the glory of the Father, so we too might walk in *newness of life....* We will certainly be united with him in a resurrection like his.... We believe that we shall also live with him. We know that Christ, being raised from the dead, will never die again; death no longer has dominion over him.... So you also must consider yourselves dead to sin and *alive to God* in Christ Jesus."

We can note at once that Paul uses two tenses. The *present* tense: "we might walk in newness of life," "alive to God in Christ Jesus"; and the *future tense:* "we will certainly be united with him," "we...shall also live with him."

Therefore the new life, too, is dynamic; it is not in effect only in the present but is a beginning of what will be fullness of life with Jesus. The two aspects—the present life and the future life—are both an organic part of being with Jesus.

* We read the same relationship between present and future in another Pauline text, which describes union with the heavenly Christ: "So if you have been raised with Christ, seek the things that are above, where Christ is, seated at the right hand of God. Set your minds on things that are above, not on things that are on earth, for you have died, and your life is hidden with Christ in God. When Christ who is your life is revealed, then you also will be revealed with him in glory" (Col 3:1-4).

There are three verbs in the present (*seek, set,* your life *is hidden* with Christ in God) yet they indicate an inner tension, a dynamic impulse toward eternity; there is one verb in the future (*you will be revealed*) to emphasize that this life is only the beginning of what will be forever.

The New Life *(meditatio)*

In the moment of the *meditatio* we seek to reflect on the present life, on what it means to be living *now* for God in Christ. We consider first of all some fundamental aspects of this *new life*; then we will dwell, in particular, on its nature as a pilgrim life.

1. The *new life* is described not only by the Apostle but also by that verse of the Gospel of Mark which we have already quoted: the disciples are called to "be with Jesus" in daily life, in everything that he does, says, and lives day by day (Mk 3:14).

In Baptism, through the work of the Holy Spirit, we

enter into the condition of Jesus, into his *sonship,* and therefore we begin to walk "no longer according to the psychic, carnal man," but with Jesus. The new life, then, consists in persevering in this journey, in following Jesus, in choosing him again each day as the absolute, definitive companion, as the one who brings about in us the fulfillment of our real identity, which is to be children of the Father.

2. What does all this mean? Let us allow ourselves to be assisted by some images: the heart, the head, the feet and the hands.

* The new life signifies being with Jesus *with our heart,* because "where your treasure is, there your heart will be also" (Lk 12:34). If your treasure is Jesus, your heart is with him. This comes about through unceasing prayer, *continual prayer.*

Even in the most ancient Christian catechesis, for example the very first letters of Paul, we find the recommendation: "Pray without ceasing" (1 Thess 5:17). We find this fundamental Christian precept also in Luke: "Then Jesus told them a parable about their need to pray always and not to lose heart" (18:1).

Since then the Christian community has asked itself what it means to pray without ceasing, and eastern monasticism developed a profound spiritual reflection on the theme.

I think that we could speak of a movement that goes from the center to the circle and from the circle to the center.

From the center to the circle, because from "condensed" prayer we go to "diffuse" prayer. "Condensed" prayer is that prayer in which we separate ourselves from everything in order to center ourselves in the mystery of God: thus the moments of the liturgy; the moments of personal, vocal, meditative prayer; the moment of the recitation of the rosary; the visit to the Blessed

Sacrament. However, of their nature these moments generate "diffuse," continual prayer, which embraces day and night, which accompanies us in the nocturnal silence and in the morning when we awaken, prayer which we find anew at every moment of our day.

The movement from the *circle to the center*, instead, begins with diffuse prayer, without waiting for condensed prayer to attain a certain expansive energy. It begins and begins again with invocations, aspirations, supplications, intercessions, thanksgiving, spread (diffused) throughout the day, so as to penetrate each circumstance of life, consciously and unconsciously if, through a gift of God, it becomes habitual.

I spoke of "gift." But we must not believe that it is a gift given only to some; rather, it is a gift proper to every Christian, because being with Jesus with the heart means being with the heart there where our treasure is.

It is thus a matter of a prayer that is possible, which we must desire, even throughout our whole life. Without unceasing prayer, condensed prayer does not attain its true depth; one facilitates the other, prepares for it, and the two are in continuity with one another.

It is a gift for which we must never cease to ask the Lord, for it allows us to be with him in the midst of all our hardships, all our preoccupations even in professional life, all the aspects of our relationships, in the difficulties of social and political commitment.

I remember that once some young priests asked me to explain to them how to live the spirit of prayer amidst the struggles of the ministry, in the multiple activities that threatened to overwhelm them. And I said this to them: if you do not strive for constant prayer, you will never find the time to set aside for condensed prayer (even though each of us, obviously, has his or her own journey of continual prayer, which corresponds to his or her own history).

When I went to Moscow for the millennium of the baptism of Rus' of Kiev, the signs of religious rebirth were already beginning to appear, and I spontaneously asked myself: How could this people, whom I see praying so fervently in church, preserve the faith if for seventy years they were deprived of any public catechesis, any communitarian expression of Christian life? And I seemed to understand that the Russian people preserved their faith partly because the liturgy continued and partly because of the influence of the monastic life and the practice of continual prayer. Certainly you are familiar with the formula of continual prayer or "prayer of the heart" born in the Eastern Church: "*Jesus, Son of God, have mercy on me a sinner.*" This formula, repeated thousands of times a day, permits us to be united to Jesus with our heart. But we can express unceasing prayer in other ways, for example, with a formula of Trinitarian prayer, in which we invoke the Father in the name of Jesus, that he might give us the gift of the Holy Spirit.

Being with Jesus in prayer will help us acquire his prayer as Son, because he always, during his earthly life and even now, pronounces the name of the Father in the Spirit.

* The new life, which we already live and which is an anticipation of eternity, of that day without end in which we will openly utter the name of the Father in the heart of Jesus and enfolded in the grace of the Spirit, means also being with Jesus with *our head*, that is, with our eyes, our ears and mouth, looking at him, listening to him, speaking his words.

With our eyes, because being with Jesus means desiring to see him, as Zacchaeus did (cf Lk 19:1-10).

With our ears, because we want to listen to him, as did the Twelve, and this is possible by means of the Gospel and the entire Bible. From this stems the invitation to learn the exercise of the *lectio divina*, which teaches us how to read the Bible by praying over it, so as to enter into the thought of Jesus, into the mysteries of his life, so as to understand that the saints, the prophets and the wise men of the Old Testament (Abraham, Isaac, Jacob, Joseph, Moses, David, Isaiah, Jeremiah, etc.) are prefigurements of Jesus. We enter, then, into the world of Jesus by means of the constant practice of the *lectio divina*, following the texts of the weekday Masses and the Sunday lectionary, then extending our meditation to the entire Scripture.

A courageous act of the Second Vatican Council was that of asking all the laity, all baptized Christians, to acquire perfect knowledge of Christ through the meditative and prayerful reading of the Bible (*DV* n. 25).

I am convinced that the *lectio divina* is a pastoral priority today, because in a sophisticated culture such as ours, only personal and direct penetration of the world of God will allow us to remain firm in the faith.

The new life also means being with Jesus *with our mouth*, because, thanks to the *lectio divina*, we learn to see and to judge reality according to the spirit of Jesus, and thus to pronounce with our mouths the words of Jesus, to speak of him, to speak like him.

* The new life is being with Jesus *with our feet*, walking with him: "Walk in newness of life" (Rom 6:4). The biblical metaphor of the journey invites us to act as Jesus acted, to love what he loved.

Jesus' way of acting, his way of journeying in life leads us to choose *poverty* and *humiliations*.

A fundamental page of the *Spiritual Exercises* of St. Ignatius expresses conformity to the behavior of Jesus with the *third degree of humility*, perfect humility, which one possesses when, "together with the first (breaking with mortal sin) and the second (breaking with venial sin, to be free of heart)...in order to imitate and resemble Christ our Lord more closely, I desire and choose poverty with the poor Christ rather than riches, injuries with the suffering Christ rather than honor, and I prefer to be esteemed stupid and crazy for Christ, who was the first to be esteemed such, rather than wise and prudent in this world" (n. 167).

The saints understood that to walk with Jesus we must not be content with the happy medium but we need to make an evangelical choice, decisively consistent with the dynamism of our baptismal commitment.

Let us think of Francis of Assisi. According to the account of Thomas of Celano, on the feast of the apostle Matthias, February 24, 1209, in the chapel of the Portiuncula, Francis listened to "those words which Jesus in the Gospel spoke to his disciples when he sent them to preach, that is, that they carry with them neither gold nor silver, neither purse nor bread nor stick for the journey, neither shoes nor two tunics. When, after an in-depth explanation by the priest, he (Francis) understood that, he was filled with indescribable joy and exclaimed: 'It is precisely that which I long to carry out with all my strength.'" Francis then understood *poverty* as an evangelical priority. And it is interesting to reread his words to his first companions: "'Early in the morning we will go in church and consult the book of the Gospels, to know what Christ taught his disciples.'(...) When on the following morning he opened the book of the Gospels, he came across the words of Christ: 'If you want to be perfect, go sell what you have and give it to the poor, and you will have treasure in heaven'; 'do not take anything for the journey.' And the saint stated: 'Brothers, here is our life and rule, and the life and rule of all those who want to join us'" (*Dizionario Francescano*, 1378-79).

The discourse on poverty has always to be repeated and is always opposed, always dismissed, always left to the side, even in the Church, because it obliges us to a radical conversion, to being with Jesus totally. The history of the Church is an attempt to continually re-conform to this priority choice, according to various forms and expressions.

Together with poverty we must choose, as St. Ignatius says, *humiliations*. I cannot cite all the texts of St. Francis on the subject, but the few I want to recall are sufficient to show how he discovered this second priority as being innate to the Gospel.

Let us think of his prayer as he contemplates Jesus: "O admirable nobility, O stupendous condescension! O sublime humility! O humble sublimity, that the Lord of the universe, God and Son of God, so humbles himself as to conceal himself, for our salvation, under the appearance of bread! Look, brothers, upon the humility of God, and open your hearts before him; humble yourselves, that he may exalt you" (*Dizionario,* 1871). Humility means being in love with Jesus, it means wanting to be with him. Therefore whoever is humble seeks, welcomes and accepts all the humiliations which the evangelical life brings.

Francis practiced humiliation with his imagination, picturing to himself embarrassing occasions and situations. He imagined himself opposed by the friars gathered in Chapter and considered a useless man, incapable, worthless and with no learning. And he played with his imagination in reconstructing the remarks and scenes: "We don't want you to rule over us, because you are not eloquent, you are simple and ignorant. In the end I am driven out with disgrace, despised by all. I say to you: if in listening to these words I do not maintain the same appearance, the same joy, the same resolution of holiness, then I am not a friar minor." The classic example is the famous story of "true and perfect happiness," which characterizes in an inimitable manner Francis' extraordinary dramatic ability and his permanent state of humility (*Dizionario,* 1892).

Perfect happiness, the fruit of poverty and humiliation, is a typical evangelical characteristic, little known not only to the world but also in Christian life. It is therefore a treasure to be rediscovered, for oneself and for others. We must always question ourselves to understand how we are living it in concrete circumstances.

* Finally there is being with Jesus *with our hands*, that is, with the various forms of active charity, of service to our neighbor, with all the lay experiences amply described in *Christifideles Laici* (*The Lay Members of Christ's Faithful People*, by John Paul II).

In the Gospel of Matthew Jesus himself, in speaking of acts of charity to various categories of persons, says: "You did it to me" (Mt 25:40). With our hands we are with him every time we make ourselves available in daily life to the least of our brothers and sisters, and even more so when this service assumes, at least internally, the quality of selflessness.

The Pilgrim Life *(meditatio)*

The new life with Jesus, today, unfolds in the fundamental dimension of journeying; it is a *pilgrim life*.

In chapter 3 of the Letter to the Colossians, Paul exhorted us to seek "the things that are above, where Christ is seated, at the right hand of God," to set our minds on "the things that are above, not on things that are on earth," for "you have died, and your life is hidden with Christ in God" (Col 3:1ff).

The life of the baptized poses a certain imbalance between earth and heaven: we are here and yet we do not feel completely at home here, we are here and yet we are on a journey toward a goal. The correct definition of a Christian is that of a pilgrim.

Pilgrims are not strangers, who find themselves outside their own country without knowing whether they will ever return. Neither are they exiles who live in sadness because they know that they will never return to their own land. Pilgrims are not vagabonds or wanderers. Pilgrims are, instead, persons who know very well where they are going and where they want to go. For this reason they live and face the uncertainties of the journey, the darkness, the complications, and even the ambiguity of the pilgrimage.

The homeland of the pilgrim is Jesus. Jesus is with us on earth, we are with him in mind and heart; but at the same time Jesus is up above and we must be with him.

If our being with Jesus is sometimes weak, not very incisive, not joyful, it probably means that we don't live this imbalance inherent to the Christian life, which means being with the Risen One near the Father. Without this holy imbalance, our humanity is weakened, is impoverished, locks itself off, becomes a prey to emotions, to success or lack of success, to being praised or despised; it becomes a prey to many fears.

How many fears there are today in the Church, how much anxiety for the future, how many complaints about what is being done or not being done! How, I ask myself, can a Christian live always regretting a past which perhaps was not very glorious? How can a Christian fear the future, almost as though the faith were in agony, almost as though Christianity had no more hope in this secularized world of ours?

The answer is found in the lack of effort to seek the essential, in not understanding or in forgetting that the Christian life is a pilgrimage.

To help us, then, acquire the truth about ourselves, that of being pilgrims journeying toward the fullness of the kingdom, I would like to briefly recall the great pilgrims whose presence marks the history of salvation.

* Hebrews 11:8-10: "By faith *Abraham* obeyed when he was called to set out for a place that he was to receive

as an inheritance; and he set out, not knowing where he was going." At the beginning of the pilgrimage of faith we start by basing ourselves on the Word of God, on his promise, without knowing what the point of arrival is, accepting the unknown and the slowness of the journey, the dark and dramatic moments, perhaps even missing the path and then finding it again because the desire to reach the goal is stronger than any other desire. "By faith (Abraham) stayed for a time in the land he had been promised, as in a foreign land, living in tents, as did Isaac and Jacob, who were heirs with him of the same promise. For he looked forward to the city that has foundations, whose architect and builder is God." Looking at the definitive city, he could remain in the tents without complaining, without becoming discouraged, knowing that the builder of that city is God.

Hebrews 11:27: "By faith *(Moses)* left Egypt," he became a pilgrim, "unafraid of the king's anger; for he persevered as though he saw him who is invisible."

Hebrews 12:2: and *we,* too, "lay aside every weight and the sin that clings so closely, and let us run with perseverance the race that is set before us, looking to Jesus the pioneer and perfecter of our faith."

The pilgrimage truly becomes a race toward the goal that is Jesus.

* The theme of the pilgrimage returns in the great saints. The writings of *St. Francis* repeat twice, to the letter, the phrase of St. Peter the apostle in which he defined Christians as "aliens and pilgrims" (1 Pet 2:11) and he exhorts them to conduct themselves as such in this world. And St. Clare, taking this thought from St. Francis' Rule, applies it to herself and to her sisters. Evidently it is not only an expression dear to St. Francis, but is above all a concept and an ideal firmly established in his mind. "For Francis, to feel oneself to be a pilgrim and exile means, positively, two things in particular: to be truly poor (therefore dispossessed, lacking every-thing, dependent, humble) and to hope with great trust in the sure providence of the Lord" (*Dizionario Teologico*, 1263, 1265).

In reading the *Autobiography* of Ignatius of Loyola we become aware that, in speaking of himself in the third person, he uses only one definition: pilgrim. This is the image that the founder of the Society of Jesus has of himself.

* Above all, I suggest for your contemplation the icon of *Mary* as pilgrim, of her who "is like a 'mirror' in which are reflected in the most profound and limpid way 'the mighty works of God' (Acts 2:11)" (*Redemptoris Mater*, n. 25).

The encyclical of John Paul II, which I have just cited, is a long meditation on that "'pilgrimage of faith' in which 'the Blessed Virgin advanced,' faithfully pre-serving her union with Christ" (n. 5). The whole Church is called to find itself in this pilgrimage, because it does not concern only the history of Mary of Nazareth, of her personal journey of faith, but "of the whole People of God, of all those who take part in the same 'pilgrimage of faith'" (n. 5). The nature of the People of God is to be, like and with Mary, a pilgrim of faith.

Again the Pope writes: "All this is accomplished in a great historical process, comparable 'to a journey.' The pilgrimage of faith indicates the interior history, that is, the story of souls. But it is also the story of all human beings, subject here on earth to transitoriness, and part of the historical dimension" (n. 6).

All of humanity is therefore led toward a very cer-tain end, which it perhaps does not understand and yet which is the dynamic force of its development, that which permits it to continually correct its errors and to recover from its failures.

We must thus look positively at the history of humanity, thinking of the goal that attracts it, of the end of the pilgrimage, which is the kingdom, the heavenly Jerusalem, Jesus. This term offers the key to the historical journey and permits us to distinguish authentic growth from decadence and degradation. The image of a pilgrimage is not linear but complex, composite: to stop, to tire, to turn back, to take the wrong road, to feel confused, to understand nothing, and then to find once more the way back.

"Here there opens up a broad prospect, within which the Blessed Virgin Mary continues to 'go before' the People of God. Her exceptional pilgrimage of faith represents a constant point of reference for the Church, for individuals, and for communities, for peoples and nations and, in a sense, for all humanity. It is indeed difficult to encompass and measure its range.

"The Council emphasizes that the Mother of God is already the eschatological fulfillment of the Church: 'In the most holy Virgin the Church has already reached that perfection whereby she exists without spot or wrinkle (cf Eph 5:27)'; and at the same time the Council says that 'the followers of Christ still strive to increase in holiness by conquering sin, and so they raise their eyes to Mary, who shines forth to the whole community of the elect as a model of virtues.'"

This is how we are with Jesus together with Mary assumed into heaven. "The pilgrimage of faith no longer belongs to the Mother of the Son of God: glorified at the side of her Son in heaven, Mary has already crossed the threshold between faith and that vision which is 'face to face' (1 Cor 13:12). At the same time, however, in this eschatological fulfillment, Mary does not cease to be the 'Star of the Sea' for all those who are still on the journey of faith" (n. 6). "Star of the Sea," as we know, is an expression used by St. Bernard in his sermon on the Nativity of Mary: "Take away this star of the sun which illumines the world and what happens to the day? Take away Mary, this *Star of the Sea*, yes of the great and immense sea, and what remains but a vast fog and the shadow of death and the darkest shadows?" Without Mary, those who make the pilgrimage of faith are lost; with Mary, always lifting our gaze to her, we can understand the truth of our journey and be comforted in moments of darkness and difficulty.

Let us ask ourselves, in prayer, how we live the new life with Jesus, and how we are pilgrims toward Jesus together with Mary, imitating their way of journeying and of living.

Being with Jesus and Mary

Overcoming the Fear of Death

"Enlighten our minds, O Lord, inflame our hearts, as you inflamed the hearts of the disciples of Emmaus, so that we may understand the glory you promise us, the life which you already give us, and the hidden mystery which you make us know through faith.

"Mary, our Mother, give us grace to understand what you are living in being with the Lord, that we may succeed in expressing it in life, in sickness, in death, in the resurrection and in glory. To attain this goal, give us, O Father, the grace of the Holy Spirit which we ask through Christ our Lord. Amen."

We have meditated on what it means concretely to be with Jesus in death and to be with him in the new life.

Now we ask ourselves what it means to be with Christ and Mary in their ascension and assumption. Translating this existentially we may say: being with Jesus and Mary in overcoming the fear of death.

Today there is little said about death and heaven, but I believe it is very important to give a place in our thoughts to the last realities which open up for us the real understanding of the meaning of earthly life and of

God's plan in history, urging us on to act with courage and enthusiasm in daily life.

I therefore present first, for our reflection, three brief affirmations so as to then offer three points for meditation.

Premises

1. The fear of death is an existential, ugly fact, in some ways impossible to eliminate; it is a guarantee of living because it mobilizes the instincts of preservation, of resistance, of vital aggressiveness.

We cannot combat the fear of death with reasoning, because it arises of itself, it is invincible.

2. The fear of death is the symbol of every other fear in the face of physical, psychic and social deprivation. Death, in fact, is the last act of the many dramas of which the human person is the protagonist: sickness, old age (especially if accompanied by infirmities and solitude), fatigue, nervous exhaustion, loss of the taste for work, for encounters, for nature; and then social deprivations, such as failures, loss of fame, of prestige, of the role we had acquired. These are all forms of anticipation of death. For this reason we experience them with fear and horror; we would rather they not happen.

3. These fears, while being morally neutral (since fear is an instinct), are in reality, however, a cause and sign of interior slavery, because they block us. For example, the fear of losing fame and esteem leads us to act differently from the way we should and want to act. The fear of losing the quiet life, comfort, pushes many persons to an indolent, negligent, sinful life. And the fear of death can drive us to experiences which are a revenge on it; I am thinking of the excesses in sexuality, alcoholism, and drugs.

For this reason the author of the Letter to the Hebrews affirms that Jesus has shared in our flesh and blood, "so that through death he might destroy the one who has the power of death, that is, the devil, and free all those who all their lives were held in slavery by the fear of death" (Heb 2:14-15). The devil holds many people in slavery all their lives, playing on their fear of death and of every kind of physical, psychic and social deprivation.

It is, therefore, necessary that the human person (and not only the Christian) reach the point not of eliminating the fear of death but of overcoming it, of overcoming the fear of everything that might bear the image of death. Without this overcoming of fear—which is the central node of existence, the risk of truth—we are not truly with Jesus.

We can cheat in many ways and, for example, pretend to do some good, to be charitable, to be concerned with others. But we cannot pretend courage in the face of death. So many times we can presume that we are self-sacrificing, that we are capable of many renunciations; however, if we are struck with a serious illness, something springs up within us that we do not succeed in dominating, thus revealing to us that we have not in reality faced and overcome the fear of dying.

We know that Francis of Assisi ardently desired the end of his days. When Francis was already very sick, Brother Elias drew to his attention the fact that perhaps the weakest brothers would be scandalized at seeing him full of joy. "They might say: 'How can he be so happy at the moment he is dying? Shouldn't he be thinking about death?'" Francis' response is an instruction for us too: "Do you remember, Brother Elias, the vision I had at Foligno? Before then I already thought frequently of my end, but since then I have been even more preoccupied in reflecting on it every day" (*Dizionario*, 1062).

Let us then seek to reflect on it, first of all by considering, through the contemplation of a biblical scene, how Jesus overcomes the fear of death; then we will see the effects of Jesus' victory; finally we will seek to point out a way for us.

Jesus Overcomes the Fear of Death

We know from memory the biblical scene which presents Jesus in the Garden of Gethsemane.

1. He is struggling with this knot of human existence which is the *anguish of death*. It may seem strange because he is the Son of God, but Jesus was afraid; he desired truly to share in our human condition, especially in our condition as sinners, because of which the end of life is clothed in remorse, extreme solitude and anxiety.

* Mark 14:33-34: He "began to be distressed and agitated. And he said to them, 'I am deeply grieved, even to death'"; it is therefore a fear which can actually kill.

We could believe that the fear of Jesus is simply fear of death in general. In reality Mark specifies that he is in anguish over *that* death: He "prayed that, if it were possible, the hour might pass from him. He said, 'Abba, Father, for you all things are possible; remove *this cup* from me'" (vv. 35-36). The cup is not simple biological death, but the concentration point of an economy of sin, cruelty, betrayal, desperation, separation from God. It is the death which man lives as a symbol of the second death. Jesus lives it and faces it as such.

* The evangelist *John,* who does not record the scene in the garden of Gethsemane, also describes Jesus struggling with this fear: "Very truly, I tell you, unless a grain of wheat falls into the earth and dies, it remains just a single grain; but if it dies, it bears much fruit. Those who love their life lose it, and those who hate their life in this world will keep it for eternal life. Whoever serves me must follow me, and where I am, there will my servant be also. Whoever serves me, the Father will honor. *Now my soul is troubled.* And what should I say—'Father, save

me from this hour'? No, it is for this reason that I have come to this hour" (Jn 12:24-27). After having spoken about the truth of death, he recognizes that he is troubled because he is about to enter into this mystery.

* The same author of the Letter to the Hebrews speaks of Jesus who "offered up prayers and supplications, *with loud cries and tears,* to the one who was able to save him from death" (Heb 5:7).

* Luke, in his turn, records the episode of Gethsemane in these terms: "In his anguish he prayed more earnestly, and his sweat became like great drops of blood falling down on the ground" (Lk 22:44). It is a psychic and biological participation so intense as to shake the whole organism.

2. *In the midst of his fear of death Jesus was consoled* because of his perseverance in prayer.

* Luke 22:43: "Then an angel from heaven appeared to him and gave him strength."

The fact that Jesus needed to be comforted and let himself be comforted, that is, strengthened, emphasizes the fact that we are truly faced with a fundamental difficulty of human experience, even if we do everything we can to remove it. When we are aware that death is near and fear assails us, we feel the need to be comforted, just as Jesus did.

* John 12:28: After Jesus invoked the Father, "a voice came from heaven, '*I have glorified it,* and I will glorify it again.'" The Father thus comforts him.

* Hebrews 5:7: "Jesus offered up prayers and supplications, with loud cries and tears, to the one who was able to save him from death, and *he was heard because of his reverent submission.*" Jesus' prayer was not answered with liberation from death but with the comfort which enabled him to overcome fear.

3. *Jesus was made perfect through this trial.* We are embarrassed to use such an expression because Jesus is

the Messiah, the Savior. However, in fact, while he was potentially perfect he became so fully and authentically, expressing all the virtuality he had already possessed, by means of the terrible trial he went through.

Hebrews 5:8-9: "Although he was a Son, he learned obedience through what he suffered; and *having been made perfect* (therefore having reached perfection), he became the source of eternal salvation for all who obey him."

We, too, are truly ourselves, truly perfect, obedient, truly sons and daughters, when we have passed through this trial, learning trust and abandonment to the Father. When everything goes well for us we can delude ourselves. Only when every exit is barred, at the moment of our death, are we confronted with the mystery of abandonment to God, of knowing how to entrust ourselves as children to the Father.

I suggest that you personally meditate again on the biblical scene of Gethsemane, because it is very rich in instruction. Jesus overcomes the fear of death at a high price; he overcomes it by facing it, by praying and letting himself be comforted by God; he overcomes it and in doing so is perfected.

The Effects of Jesus' Victory

Jesus' victory over death is the source from which the experience of the saints springs forth.

* First of all, let us read some texts from *Paul.*

The Apostle is in prison, he has suffered persecution, there are people who oppose him by preaching Jesus in a spirit of rivalry, with intentions that are not honest, and so he lives a kind of anticipation of death.

However, Paul is certain that *everything has meaning:* "I know that through your prayers and the help of the Spirit of Jesus Christ this will turn out for my deliverance. It is my eager expectation and hope that I will not be put to shame in any way, but that by my speaking with all boldness, Christ will be exalted now as always in my body, whether by life or death" (Phil 1:19-20). He has overcome the fear of death by giving meaning to imprisonment, to humiliation, and by growing in hope. For this reason he can say: "For to me, living is Christ and *dying is gain*" (v. 21). The ardent desire arises in him to *"depart and be with Christ"* (v. 23), a desire which is evidently joined with availability to whatever God wants.

Again in Philippians (2:17-18) his victory over death appears: "But even if I am poured out as a libation" (he foresees his martyrdom) "over the sacrifice and the offering of your faith, I am glad and rejoice with all of you— and in the same way you also must be glad and rejoice with me." These words of the Apostle are a very clear sign of the baptismal resurrection that has taken possession of his spirit.

In 2 Corinthians 12:10, he is content "with weaknesses, insults, hardships, persecutions, and calamities for the sake of Christ; for whenever I am weak, then I am strong."

The human person instinctively represses anguish (suffice it to think of all the medicine consumed today so as to avoid pain, not to face it). But Paul has so integrated in himself the victory of Jesus that he is content with his weaknesses, seeing them as a sign of God's strength— whether these weaknesses are physical (infirmities), social (affronts), religious (persecutions), psychic (anguish).

* Let us contemplate in other saints this extraordinary image of victory over death. In his Letter to the Romans *St. Ignatius of Antioch* writes: "It is better for me to die for Jesus Christ than to extend my empire to the ends of the earth.... It is close to the moment of my birth. Let me attain pure light; once there, I will be truly a man. Let me imitate the passion of my God. I write to you that

I desire to die. Every earthly desire of mine is crucified and there is no longer any longing in me for material goods, but a living water murmurs within me and says: Come to the Father" (cf chapters 6:1-9).

Francis of Assisi calls the victory over death "perfect happiness." For Francis, perfect happiness is to share, through suffering, in the sufferings of Christ, so as to become participants in his glory which is the cross, in which lies the supreme revelation of God's love; and it is pure happiness in faith before the glory of Jesus. He attains perfect happiness through prolonged suffering: in a torment of doubt about his choice; in the beginning but especially, for a longer time, when he sees the wide gap between his "utopia" and the concrete reality of those who followed him. The distance between the utopia and the reality can destroy, because it makes him understand how mediocrity, negligence, everything that belongs to death's field of influence, takes away from man the possibility of attaining his real end.

Francis is therefore tempted to give the Order back to God, as if it were "something of his" which had ended badly. God relieves him by questioning and admonishing him: "Why are you disturbed, little man?" Francis overcame all this anguish, and perfect happiness led him to desire death: "Since the servant of God desired to enter into the temple of divine glory, the Lord called him to himself, and so he passed from this world to the Father" (cf *Dizionario*, 2185-2186).

The *Canticle of the Creatures* is a stupendous expression of the victory obtained over death.

Among the many other saints whom we could recall, I will limit myself to some thoughts on Monica and Augustine. They are at Ostia, alone, leaning out a window overlooking the garden of the house where they are guests: "We then conversed with great sweetness. Forgetting those things that were past and straining forward to those that were before, we inquired of one another, in the presence of the truth which You are, what the eternal life of the saints would be like, which eye has not seen, nor ear heard, nor has it occurred to the heart of man. With the mouth of our heart we were longing for the supreme wave of your fount, the fount of life which is with you, so that we could be bathed in it according to our capacity, we could in some way conceive of a reality that is so lofty.... And ascending in ourselves through the consideration of your works, we reached our own minds and even transcended them so as to attain the region of inexhaustible abundance, where you nourish Israel eternally with the food of truth, where life is Wisdom, through which all things present, past and future are made. This Wisdom itself is not made but is as it was and as it ever will be.... And as we spoke of it and longed for it, we attained to it somewhat with the total effort of our mind, and while sighing we left behind, bound to it, the first fruits of the spirit" (*Confessions* IX, ch. 10:23-24).

For Monica, especially, the fear of death is overcome, and she says: "My son, for my part, this life no longer has any attraction for me. I do not know what I am still doing here and why I am here. My hopes on this earth have been fulfilled" (26).

* In the yearning of Paul, Ignatius, Francis, and Monica, we must read the sentiments of Mary. She, in fact, looked forward, during the slow passage of time, to the unspeakable joy of seeing her Son again. She desired with all the ardor of her heart to contemplate the face of God unveiled, to be forever in the arms of the Father. She serenely waited for her earthly life to be concluded as the last form of her initial abandonment: "Let it be with me according to your word" (Lk 1:38).

The Journey toward Overcoming the Fear of Death

How, then, can we overcome that crucial knot of the

person's life, to which all the other knots are fastened, that is, the fear of death?

1. First of all, we need to say that it is a lifelong journey and that no one can know what their emotional, psychological and affective reactions will be at the moment of trial and death. We must therefore always remain humble and recognize our fragility.

2. Overcoming the fear of death is not accomplished through our human efforts but first of all by being with Jesus and Mary who have already overcome all fear.

Being with Jesus and Mary means praying so as not to fall into temptation (cf Lk 23:46), the temptation to lose faith and hope which is hurled at us, so to speak, by trial and by death. "Lord, do not let us fall into temptation, into the temptation of losing faith in the face of death. Unite our prayer to that of Jesus in the garden, grant us abandonment in you."

We can repeat the formulas which the Church has handed down for centuries: "Passion of Christ, strengthen me. Do not let me be separated from you. From the evil enemy defend me. In the hour of my death call me and bid me come to you, to praise you with your saints forever." We can recite the "Hail Mary," while thinking of our own death: "Pray for us now and at the hour of our death."

In doing this we will dispose ourselves to the fulfillment of the baptismal dynamism which is fully realized at the moment of death.

3. Overcoming the fear can be made possible now in hope, can be tasted in the grace, whether implicit or explicit, of the contemplation of our heavenly dwelling.

In the Letter to the Romans, as we have seen, Paul speaks of "dying to sin," to "be buried with Christ," so as to "rise with Jesus, walking in newness of life." In the Letter to the Ephesians he adds a third element because, after having said: "even when we were dead through our trespasses, (God) made us alive together with Christ...and raised us up with him," he writes: "(he) seated us with him in the heavenly places in Christ Jesus" (2:5-6). It is the application of the mystery of the ascension to us: we *are already* in heaven, we have overcome death. This means that in Paul and in the community of Ephesus the reflection on baptismal dynamism is developed to the point of the ascension of Jesus and the assumption of Mary. While we are still on this earth, we are within the sphere of action of the Risen One. The exegete *Heinrich Schlier,* in his commentary on the Letter to the Ephesians, explains how Christians, united in Christ, have with Christ *transcended themselves* in what concerns their being and their person (therefore even the fear of death) because Baptism is like an ascension into heaven. The Church is above all in heaven: through Baptism the faithful are in and with Christ in his Body the Church—Jews and Gentiles—and his body is in heaven.

We can thus contemplate the Church in its ascending aspect, in its difficult journey toward the fullness of the kingdom, and we can fruitfully contemplate its descending aspect: the Church is already there, in its Head, it is in heaven in Mary, in the Apostles, in the saints, and it descends with all its strength so as to conquer history.

It is a very useful vision, even for overcoming the many problems of institutional tensions. The Church's temporal journey is secondary, it is relative with respect to its truth which is in heaven. When we say the Church we mean all of redeemed humanity which, in Jesus, is already with God; it has already conquered the powers of the world, the excessive power of the world closed within itself, the atmosphere of sin, dishonesty, indifference, secularism. On earth the Church fights against these negative realities, having already conquered them in Christ in whom the Church lives.

We must not be frightened by the evil, by the disbelief which seems to be on the increase, for Christ is not frightened because he has already conquered sin, has already conquered and overcome the fear of death and of all the forces that enslave the human person.

In faith and in hope, not in visibility, has the victory come about.

For this reason, in the Letter to the Colossians Paul can say: "So if you have been raised with Christ, seek the things that are above, where Christ is, seated at the right hand of God" (Col 3:1). Our center of gravity is in heaven. "Set your minds on things that are above, not on things that are on earth, for you have died," you have been rescued from the evil dynamism of worldliness and "your life is hidden with Christ in God. When Christ who is your life is revealed, then you also will be revealed with him in glory" (vv. 2-4).

This life is one of faith and of hope, but no less real for this reason. In fact, it is so real that when Christ is manifested, we will be manifested fully in that which we already are. Herein lies the possibility of resisting the lures of evil, the temptations to diffidence, fear, desperation and discouragement. Thinking continually of our true place, which is being with Jesus at the right hand of the Father, we dominate all worldly powers.

This contemplation to which we are called as Christians is the only one that allows us to live the truth of ourselves. Anything less than this implies a Christian existence that is weak, shrunken, melancholic, undeveloped.

Conclusion

I would like to conclude by citing the passage of a letter written by St. Clare to St. Agnes of Bohemia, in which she invites her to enter into the dynamic of the paschal mystery lived in Baptism:

"If you suffer with him, you will reign with him. If

you weep with him, you will rejoice with him. If in his company you die on the cross of tribulation, you will possess with him the heavenly dwelling in the splendor of the saints. Therefore you will possess for all eternity and for all centuries the glory of the heavenly kingdom, in place of earthly honors which are so fleeting; you will share in eternal goods instead of perishable goods; you will live forever and ever" (Clare of Assisi, *Letter to Blessed Agnes of Prague*).

I believe that, more than ever, the Church today needs to reflect on the dynamism of baptism so as not to retire within limited horizons. If, out of negligence or accommodation to the world, we deprive ourselves of the global picture of faith (which Paul always had clearly in mind), if we dismiss it or take it for granted, we will end up toiling and wearing ourselves out in the petty realities of daily life and we will lose heart.

May Mary, who believed above and beyond all reasoning, help us so that we may possess the Truth in Jesus. Her assumption incarnates the hope of the world, enlightens the Christian journey by teaching us how all earthly vicissitudes should be contemplated in the light of eternity, in an ever increasing impetus of faith and hope.

Let us therefore pray for one another, asking the Lord to overcome the pure verbalism of words and, in the grace of Christ, to attain knowledge of the Truth.

Christian Witness in a Broken World

(Homily for the Twenty-first Sunday in Ordinary Time)

The three readings of this twenty-first Sunday of Ordinary Time allow us to allude to three important themes within the ambit of our retreat.

The first is the *personalization of faith*, in relation to the first reading from the Book of Joshua.

The second is the *relationship between matrimony and consecrated virginity* in view of the kingdom, in relation to the second reading from the Letter to the Ephesians.

The third is the problem of *non-belief* today, in relation to the gospel passage of John.

The Personalization of Faith

Joshua said to the whole people of Israel: "Choose this day whom you will serve" (Josh 24:1-2, 15-17, 18).

The proposal seems strange. Isn't the Lord the only one whom we should serve? How can we choose between serving God and serving idols? And how even discern between the idols whom their fathers served beyond the river, those of the land of Mesopotamia, and the gods of the Amorites?

Certainly it doesn't refer to such a choice, but to that process of personalization of faith by means of which the word of God, proposed and offered, the communication God makes of himself, can become a personal response, thus a choice.

The theme of personalization of faith is fundamental today for the whole western world, for a world which has passed, in some way, to a more advanced age, and no longer allows itself to be led by criteria of ambient, of authority, of fidelity to the group. Perhaps in centuries past, beginning from the fourth or fifth century, there were conversions in which the "group principle" was also at work (there were times in which one could refer to the conversion of the king or the head of a tribe). In our western civilization which is so diversified in its traditions, so divided in its opinions, there is the occasion for a unique maturation of the faith.

Thus, personalization of faith is needed. Each Christian has to carry out the journey so as to integrate the faith with his or her own individuality through decisive and courageous choices.

This is what it means to be *lay persons*. It is not enough to receive Baptism; we need to commit ourselves to an itinerary of personalization of faith, which enables us to acquire an adult faith. This is where the various ministries and services within the Christian people come from, so as to foster a faith which expresses the holiness of the Christian today. I see the meaning of your charism, as that of every secular institute, precisely in this capacity for personal commitment and for attracting others so that they, too, make a choice of radical evangelical faith that corresponds to the baptismal dynamism.

Note that the people of Israel, challenged by Joshua, make a motivated choice: "Far be it from us that we should forsake the Lord to serve other gods; for it is the Lord our God who brought us and our ancestors up from the land of Egypt, out of the house of slavery, and who did these great signs in our sight. He protected us along all the way that we went, and among all the peoples through whom we passed" (Josh 24:16-17).

It is thus not a matter of a response given simply out of habit (we have always done it this way, our parents taught us to behave this way, it is a tradition in our families to be Christians). The people assimilated the Word, the gifts of God, and responded personally.

Therefore I consider it your task, even in the diverse realities in which you live, to promote personalization of faith through the example of your life and by means of your specific journey of radicalness in the response of faith.

Matrimony and Celibacy for the Kingdom

The passage from the Letter to the Ephesians (cf Eph 5:21-32) speaks of matrimony, but, as we well know, the theme is treated in direct relationship to the Lord and the Church.

Thus there is present in marriage a dynamism which causes it to rise from the natural, biological reality to a moral, more properly spousal reality, and finally to a reality of grace and submission, of communion with Christ, so as to represent the highest spousal reality of the Church, that is, the choice of Christ as the only Lord.

If marriage has this intrinsic dynamic force, so that it is not saved even on a human level (especially in a redeemed humanity which still bears signs of its fragility) except by means of this dynamism, we can understand that the dynamism of the celibate life for the kingdom not only constitutes a different choice (or a generically better choice) but represents and expresses that dynamism of grace and of submission to Christ the only Lord, of growth in personal love for him, which is also inherent in the dynamism of marriage.

Therefore the Church *needs* the charism of celibacy,

precisely so as to assist married life, to be salt and a stimulus to it, just as the married life reminds us that the reality of the celibate is *to be* for the Lord and yet must also express itself in acts of loving service for the entire body of Christ.

Non-Belief Today

Finally the gospel passage emphasizes the theme of unbelief. Today, in the western countries (Europe and North America), we find ourselves faced more and more with a growing indifference. It is not so much a problem of atheism as that of difficulty in believing, of the inability to believe. The page from the Gospel offers us some important indications as to how we must conduct ourselves in this situation: not simply deploring the lack of belief or opposing it in a general way, but attempting to penetrate it.

"When many of his disciples heard it, they said, 'This teaching is difficult; who can accept it?'" (Jn 6:60). First of all, the temptation not to believe is a temptation for many, not just for a few. It is thus not far removed from us, it is not just for others but is also within us. We are invited to unmask it, to clarify it, and to overcome it in ourselves.

"This teaching is difficult": the temptation begins with believing a certain teaching to be disagreeable (whether about Christ, about the mystery of God, about the Church), believing it not feasible in daily experience. It is the worst temptation against faith: how do we make this teaching accord with our life, with our experience of evil, of suffering, of the uselessness of human efforts, of the suffering of the poor and the innocent?

Jesus responds by pointing out the means for facilitating our understanding of the faith.

He says first of all: "Does this offend you?" Does the difference between your discourse and mine seem too hard to accept? "Then what if you were to see the Son of Man ascending to where he was before?" It is the invitation to broaden our vision. Often difficulties in the faith arise from the fact that human views are confronted with faith views but on restricted ground. We must, instead, compare the horizons of human destinies with the broad horizons of God. At times polemics or apologetics become lost in sectorial battles, and people remain disturbed and confused. It is therefore important, very important, to offer the vision of faith in its wholeness.

This is not all, for Jesus adds: "It is the Spirit that gives life." Without the gift of the Spirit, faith is proposed only through reasoning, reflection and verbal replies. It is the mystery of the Spirit that gives life.

A mystery that collides with our resistance: "'Among you there are some who do not believe.' For Jesus knew from the first who were the ones that did not believe." Beyond the difficulties of grasping the level of the discourse of faith, the difficulties due to limited human nature, there is the resistance of human sinfulness which does not want to accept the Spirit, which does not want to allow itself to be drawn above itself, which does not want to go beyond itself, in short, does not want to make the journey of humility and listening. Here lurks the deepest resistance. Because of this, the acts of humility and of humiliation are strictly linked with the openness of the heart to faith; while all the acts of self-sufficiency and haughtiness cannot be touched even by an infinity of reasons.

And again, Jesus says: "For this reason I have told you that no one can come to me unless it is granted by the Father." Faith is a grace; it is the Father who draws a person. We must, therefore, always intercede for our faith and that of others, that the Lord may give us the daily bread of the ability to believe and to accept the presence of God in all the happy and sad circumstances of our lives and of the life of the Church and of society.

Finally we must not become frightened even if many turn back. Sometimes we are seized with panic and ask ourselves: how many will still believe in the year 2000? in 2020, in 2040? Sociologists venture some estimates and statistics. Jesus does not concern himself about this, and if many of his followers turn back, he does not lower the cost, he is not assailed by fear; in fact, he asks the Twelve: "Do you also wish to go away?"

Jesus makes us return to the fact that faith is a personal decision, not simply external adherence to please someone or to be consistent with ourselves; it means choosing the Lord, it means consenting to the love of God: a choice which, when it is resolute and strong, even if it is made by a few, is of value for many. The Twelve, the only ones who have the courage to respond: "You have the words of eternal life," are the salvation of many. Every decisive act of faith we make is worth more than one hundred acts of disbelief or fear made around us. When we decide to do something, we are much more capable of making an impression on the secularized or incredulous world in which we live.

I urge you to understand in depth your mission in this troubled society, not to allow yourselves to be frightened, but rather to take courage from the fact that many turn back, because it means that the Lord is asking of us a more intense decision of faith, and that through our decision he wants to save many others.

"Your words, Lord Jesus, are spirit and life. In giving us your body in this Eucharist, you will fill us with your Holy Spirit, and we will be able to participate in the mystery of your death and resurrection. Amen."

Part Two
Troubled Families in the Bible

❖ ❖ ❖

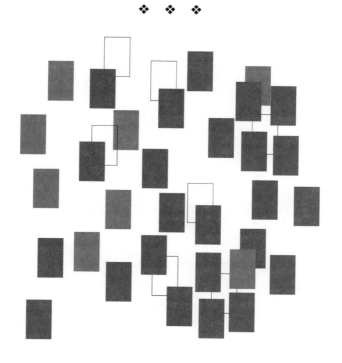

Introduction

"We thank you, Father, for granting us some moments of silence, recollection and prayer. We want to let ourselves be led by your Son Jesus to a solitary place, to listen to and speak with him. We bring with us not only our own families but the whole Church and, in particular, the problems of all the families of the world. Accept, Father, this time of silence and listening as prayer, praise, intercession and supplication especially for the families experiencing greater trials or difficulties. May our trials and problems be united to those of Mary, Joseph and Jesus, in a journey of sanctity and joy that reaches all human families. Grant that we may participate once more in the mystery of the changing of water into wine that took place at Cana, through the action of your Son. Receive the poor water of our prayers, of our recollection, of the effort to forget the many thoughts that at this moment occupy our imagination or trouble our emotions. Accept our sacrifice as humble water which, springing forth from our hearts, waits to be transformed into the wine of conjugal, familial, evangelical and eternal charity. We ask this through the intercession of Mary who was the first to intercede for this transformation. We ask this in union with all the saints in heaven and on earth, through Christ our Lord. Amen."

Premise

What do I propose to do during this brief spiritual retreat?

Assisted by your experience, I intend to think, pray, and intercede with you for all the families who live in situations of difficulty and struggle. Recently a missionary from a very poor area of Brazil wrote to me that only 10% of the people there marry in church. The other couples live together for a while, then separate and enter into other temporary unions. Obviously the whole life of the country is affected by this. Not only in Europe, then, where we breathe the atmosphere of religious indifference, consumerism or materialism, but in all parts of the world families are divided. Suffice it to think of the customs and traditions of the African countries, which hinder understanding of the Christian concept of the family.

Precisely for this reason I think it useful that our prayer be aided by reflection on the Word of God, in the desire to find, so to speak, the troubled families in the Bible. I believe that your dedicated journey of matrimonial spirituality will also benefit from this.

In fact, Sacred Scripture does not hide the negative elements, the elements of crisis present in so many families. The genealogy of Jesus which begins the Gospel according to Matthew, recalls families who were certainly not exemplary; and the genealogy of Jesus according to Luke, going back to Adam, recalls for us a large number of couples in difficulty, or of misunderstandings among brothers and sisters or between children and parents.

The first couple in crisis is Adam and Eve; not only do they not understand one another, but they accuse one another, and each attributes to the other the responsibility for the sin. These two parents then do not succeed in teaching their sons to love one another, and so we have the tragic crime of Cain against Abel.

In Noah's family the sons do not know how to respect the father. Abraham, for his part, is unable to create peace around him, whether between Sarai and Hagar, or with regard to his nephew Lot, from whom he must separate. The family of Jacob is a theater of struggles and blood, of the brothers against Joseph.

Miriam and Aaron join forces to oppose their brother Moses. The family of David is stained first by his adultery and homicide, then by the rebellion of Absalom who turns against his father, and finally by all the hatred, killing, and family vendettas recorded in the Books of Kings and of Chronicles. And then there are the misfortunes of Tobit and Job with their respective wives.

I have cited only some of the troubled families who appear throughout the whole of biblical history. Paradoxically we must include the family of Jesus, in which moments of crisis were not lacking: there is the suffering of Joseph who, at a certain point, wants to send Mary away in secret; there is the lack of comprehension on the part of Mary and Joseph about the vocation of their twelve-year-old son, when he remains in the Temple in Jerusalem.

Probably, the examples of difficult family relationships in the Bible are more numerous than those that are smooth, positive, and serene.

Six Types of Troubled Families

A spontaneous question arises: why does the Bible, which is the book of God, the book of humankind, recount the story of these families?

Certainly in order to teach us that the life of the couple, of the family, is an arduous undertaking, and that there are few persons who succeed in living it without struggles, struggles which can even be tragic and lead to ruptures and separations, whether visible or invisible.

It is against this kind of real background that Sacred Scripture constructs the ideal of Christian matrimony, of the Christian relationship of the couple. The Bible does this by beginning not from an abstract ideology but from a very difficult concrete situation, such as that which human history manifests and which even today cultures and civilizations manifest (we think of the surveys and studies on the conditions of the family in various nations).

The Bible knows that family life is difficult and because of this it wants to help us with the examples of troubled families, in such a way that we can draw comfort, indications, suggestions, and encouragement for the ideal proposed by Christian marriage.

I have chosen this theme for our reflections as I consider it important not so much for you who are living a particularly intense spiritual training so as to face the difficult moments of family life, but rather in view of the help you can offer that enormous number of families who suffer, who are inhibited by their inability to communicate, by misunderstandings that last even for decades.

Each of us, by virtue of the mission entrusted to us in Baptism, is responsible for all the others. And you, by virtue of your participation in the *Equipe Notre Dame*, are responsible not only for your own families but for all the other families spread throughout the world.

Returning to the biblical pages I have noted, I ask myself: is it possible to bring to light, from all the examples of troubled families in the Bible, a kind of typology that will allow us to classify them?

I believe that all the types are present but these six are the most important.

1. The type in which *the relationship of a couple is threatened from within* by misunderstanding or difference in viewpoint.

2. The type in which *the relationship of a couple is threatened from without* by infidelity, betrayals, or the intervention of other persons.

3. The type in which crisis enters a family because of *misunderstanding between parents and children,* like two groups that oppose one another.

4. The type in which a crisis in the family is due to *lack of understanding among the children.* One of the most frequent cases today is that of a son or daughter who follows a wrong road or enters the world of drugs, thus provoking a break with his or her brothers and sisters.

5. The type consisting in the difficult relationship between *family and society;* the family is close-knit within but feels estranged from social life. Here we are speaking of a suffering that was less frequent in ancient society, but the Bible does not ignore it. The family of Lot, for example, is in serious difficulty because of the wicked environment of Sodom, and finds itself isolated.

6. The sixth type is the most important, the one we read about at the beginning of Sacred Scripture: where the relationship of a couple or a family enters into crisis because *its relationship with God is in crisis.*

I wish to observe that some types, present in our times, are not treated in depth in the Bible. For example, all the examples related to the fear or the rejection of life reflect a morality, particularly western, which contrasts strongly with the extraordinary love for life, for offspring, for children, for the future, that characterizes the biblical mentality and tradition.

Naturally it is not possible for us to reflect upon or even look at all the types I have indicated. For the rest, my intention is not to consider several biblical episodes, but rather to demonstrate a method for deeper reflection and study, to offer a guide for interpretation which you can then use in your shared meditation and in groups.

I have chosen two stories, one of a couple and one of a family, which describe difficult situations relevant today:

* the story of *Job,* which shows a crisis in the couple's relationship;

* the story of the *family of Jacob,* in which emerges a crisis in the relationship between parents and children and among the children themselves.

A *Lectio Divina*

In offering the meditations I will follow the classical method of the *lectio divina* in its three moments.

After the *rereading* of the biblical text, we will seek to grasp the *message* that comes from it, the solutions offered to family problems. I will then offer some suggestions for the moment of *contemplation (contemplatio)* and prayer. This contemplative prayer consists especially in silence and adoration, since in any biblical scene we seek to contemplate the one who is the Word, that is, Jesus; Jesus in the presence of the Father in the Spirit and Jesus in his Body which is the Church. The suggestions that I will give will help you to understand, for example, in what way the relationship between Jesus and humankind is evidenced in the text we have read; in what way the relationship between Jesus and the Church is articulated; what crises, what sufferings, what remedies emerge from the Bible through the relationship Christ-humankind, Christ-Church; what aspects of the biblical passage shed light on our contemplation of the mystery of the three Persons in the Trinity (a communion reflected in conjugal and family life).

It might be very useful if each of you communicated to me in writing the responses or reflections which the first meditation arouses, so as to enrich and stimulate the journey of faith and prayer that we want to make. On my part I will respond to your letters in a dialogue, with practical instruction.

"O Lord, bless and fill with your presence these moments that we have set aside for listening to your Word. Fill them with the consolation of the Spirit, with the presence of Mary and of your Son Jesus; fill them with your purifying grace. Grant that the fatigue and wounds that we accumulate every day be treated, healed, cured, lifted, comforted. Accept our sacrifices as intercession for the suffering, inadequacy and failures of so many couples, of so many family situations. Grant that we be as you want us to be, free and obedient, humble and conscious of the mission you have entrusted to us in your plan for the salvation of humankind. Amen."

Bear the Trial Together

"O Lord, in the history of salvation which is proposed to us again and again in your Sacred Scripture, you have spoken to us not only of admirable relationships of communion among persons, in particular of couples and of families. You willed that in this Book of life and holiness there should also appear occasions of misunderstanding, struggle, break-up, tragedy, and hatred. We know that in this way you want to tell us that you understand us, that you support, encourage and urge us on. Grant that we may draw comfort and light from meditation on your servant Job, to help ourselves and many other families. We ask you this with Mary through Christ your Son and our Lord, in the grace of the Holy Spirit. Amen."

In this first meditation we will refer especially to the first two chapters of the Book of Job, which describe the figure of a couple who do not know how to bear the trial together; it is thus a case of a troubled family.

Job 1:1 - 2:10

"There was once a man in the land of Uz whose name was Job. That man was blameless and upright, one who feared God and turned away from evil. There were born to him seven sons and three daughters. He had seven thousand sheep, three thousand camels, five hundred yoke of oxen, five hundred donkeys, and very many servants; so that this man was the greatest of all the people of the east. His sons used to go and hold feasts in one another's houses in turn; and they would send and invite their three sisters to eat and drink with them. And when the feast days had run their course, Job would send and sanctify them, and he would rise early in the morning and offer burnt offerings according to the number of them all; for Job said, 'It may be that my children have sinned, and cursed God in their hearts.' This is what Job always did.

"One day the heavenly beings came to present themselves before the Lord, and Satan also came among them. The Lord said to Satan, 'Where have you come from?' Satan answered the Lord, 'From going to and fro on the earth, and from walking up and down on it.' The Lord said to Satan, 'Have you considered my servant Job? There is no one like him on the earth, a blameless and upright man who fears God and turns away from evil.' Then Satan answered the Lord, 'Does Job fear God for nothing? Have you not put a fence around him and his house and all that he has, on every side? You have blessed the work of his hands, and his possessions have increased in the land. But stretch out your hand now, and touch all that he has, and he will curse you to your face.' The Lord said to Satan, 'Very well, all that he has is in your power; only do not stretch out your hand against him!' So Satan went out from the presence of the Lord.

"One day when his sons and daughters were eating and drinking wine in the eldest brother's house, a messenger came to Job and said, 'The oxen were plowing and the donkeys were feeding beside them, and the Sabeans fell on them and carried them off, and killed the servants with the edge of the sword; I alone have escaped to tell you.' While he was still speaking, another came and said, 'The fire of God came from heaven and burned up the sheep and the servants, and consumed them; I alone have escaped to tell you.' While he was still speaking, another came and said, 'The Chaldeans formed three columns, made a raid on the camels and carried them off, and killed the servants with the edge of the sword; I alone have escaped to tell you.' While he was still speaking, another came and said, 'Your sons and daughters were eating and drinking wine in their eldest brother's house, and suddenly a great wind came across the desert, struck the four corners of the house, and it fell on the young people; I alone have escaped to tell you.'

"Then Job arose, tore his robe, shaved his head, and fell on the ground and worshipped. He said, 'Naked I came from my mother's womb, and naked shall I return there; the Lord gave, and the Lord has taken away; blessed be the name of the Lord.'

"In all this Job did not sin or charge God with wrong-doing.

"One day the heavenly beings came to present themselves before the Lord, and Satan also came among them to present himself before the Lord. The Lord said to Satan, 'Where have you come from?' Satan answered the Lord, 'From going to and fro on the earth, and from walking up and down on it.' The Lord said to Satan, 'Have you considered my servant Job? There is no one like him on the earth, a blameless and upright man who fears God and turns away from evil. He still persists in his integrity, although you incited me against him, to destroy him for no reason.' Then Satan answered the Lord, 'Skin for skin! All that people have they will give to save their lives. But stretch out your hand now and touch his bone and his flesh, and he will curse you to your face.' The Lord said to Satan, 'Very well, he is in your power; only spare his life.'

"So Satan went out from the presence of the Lord,

and inflicted loathsome sores on Job from the sole of his foot to the crown of his head. Job took a potsherd with which to scrape himself, and sat among the ashes.

"Then his wife said to him, 'Do you still persist in your integrity? Curse God, and die.' But he said to her, 'You speak as any foolish woman would speak. Shall we receive the good at the hand of God and not receive the bad?' In all this Job did not sin with his lips."

The Personages of This Passage

During the moment of the *lectio*, we ask ourselves first of all who are the *personages* who figure in these two chapters. Principally there are four:

* *Job,* a man who does not belong to the chosen people. His *moral figure* is already described in verse 1: a man "blameless and upright, one who feared God and turned away from evil." Then his *family* is described: seven sons and three daughters; here the number ten indicates a certain completeness, a fullness of family happiness. And, again, his *wealth* is underscored: "He had seven thousand sheep, three thousand camels" (ten thousand in all), "five hundred yoke of oxen, five hundred donkeys" (one thousand in all), "and very many servants; so that this man was the greatest of all the people of the east."

Thus Job is morally exemplary, happy in his family and fortunate in his possessions.

We also find in him a real and profound *fatherhood;* he has a great sense of the creaturely poverty of the human person and therefore of the fragility of his children. For this reason, at the conclusion of the feast days which his sons celebrated in turn, he sent for his children to sanctify them. He did not oppose their style of living, but after they had entertained themselves with these festive reunions, "he would arise early in the morning and offer burnt offerings according to the number of them all; for Job said, 'It may be that my children have sinned, and cursed God in their hearts'" (1:5). Job's is an extraordinary fatherhood: a man just, upright, not despotic, who while not impeding his children's celebrations, is aware of what can take place during feasts. With a patient and compassionate soul, with sorrowful but at the same time respectful words, he calls the children to purification.

* It is surprising that in this scene of father and children, united in a relationship of freedom and understanding, the mother, *the wife, does not appear.* Only in chapter 2, in the moment of greatest trial, does she emerge from the shadows to provoke and insult her husband. Probably she is not mentioned from the very beginning of the narrative because she would have been incapable of helping Job. If it is true that, according to eastern custom, the woman should remain somewhat hidden, in this case it seems clear that she had not achieved personal growth, she did not have strength of soul.

We ask ourselves: did Job do everything possible to communicate his inner richness to his wife? Perhaps he did and perhaps he did not. It could be that the fault is all the woman's; however, if he did not take care to weave together the loosened threads of communication, to help her to grow spiritually, we could not approve of him, even with all the merits we have already recognized in him. I know great personalities who do not succeed in establishing with their wives or husbands an equal relationship, and who keep their gifts to themselves. Naturally, ever-growing difficulties then arise between them.

In any case Job is described as a somewhat solitary man who has not accustomed his wife to share joys and sorrows.

* The third personage is *Satan,* presented to us in mysterious terms. He does not appear as the sworn enemy of God, one who does not even want to look God in the face. He appears before the Lord along with the children of God, the angels, and gives him some suggestions, even if of a provocative nature. Clearly his is the figure of an envious and pessimistic person; so we recognize how, through the urging of a malevolent and bitter force, evil enters into the heart of families, especially into a couple's relationship.

Satan does not tolerate all the good Job has done; he is suspicious of it, he does not believe that disinterested, selfless love can exist; he does not believe that Job truly loves God above the material riches and children God has given him: "Does Job fear God for nothing? Have you not put a fence around him and his house and all that he has, on every side? You have blessed the work of his hands, and his possessions have increased in the land. But stretch out your hand now, and touch all that he has, and he will curse you to your face" (1:9-11).

It is interesting that this kind of pessimism about human nature, this doubt about the person's capacity to love, has been present since the Book of Genesis. The serpent as tempter acts, in fact, by instilling in the woman the suspicion that God wants to dominate, that God has forbidden Adam and Eve to eat the fruit of a certain tree because he does not want them to become like him. "God knows that when you eat of it your eyes will be opened, and you will be like God, knowing good and evil" (Genesis 3:5).

As we know from the serpent in Genesis, Satan, as presented to us in the Book of Job, shows us how the relationship of a couple (and family relationships in general) is undermined by subtle sentiments, that is, by the fear that the other person has individual interests, secondary purposes, that such a person does not love truly and selflessly.

When doubt and suspicion enter, then the relationship begins to fall to pieces, or better, it is placed in crisis, it is put to the test.

* Another important figure, even if he remains in the background, is *God*. God loves Job and has confidence in him. God knows that the man is capable of gestures of disinterested love and he wagers on this, just as Satan wagers that a real religious spirit does not exist in the human creature.

The two wagers concern both the individual and the couple. At bottom the family is God's wager about the ability of two persons, and then more than two persons, to love one another without scheming or selfishness. The whole journey of the Christian family hinges on this, while narrow visions of the couple are based on convenience, on the return of what is given—*"I give so you will give"*—and lead to the rupture of the relationship when it no longer pays.

Thus right from the beginning the story of Job presents the problem very well by focusing on it: are marriage and the family a fruit of love, or rather of egoism and convenience?

Actions of a Very Serious Temptation

In the simple rereading of the text it is always possible to grasp, in addition to the description of the persons, some events or *actions*.

We are especially struck by the actions of a very serious *temptation*.

Job is tried in his material goods, in his fortune, in his possessions; he is tried in his children, and finally in his own person: "Satan inflicted loathsome sores on Job from the sole of his foot to the crown of his head. Job took a potsherd with which to scrape himself, and sat among the ashes" (2:7-8). The story skims over the paradox because this man is very quickly deprived of everything. Yet it is well gauged for the purpose it wants to achieve, that is, to underscore the wager as to the existence or non-existence of selfless love, even when the person remains with absolutely nothing.

How will Job behave in this terrible trial, and how will his wife and friends act, those who ought to help him? The whole Book develops this theme, and I suggest—because of its usefulness and its teachings—that you reread it, even during the days following our retreat.

The Fundamental Words of the Text

I limit myself to recalling the fundamental words which concern us more closely, that is, those of Job and his wife.

Deprived of his wealth and his children, "Job arose, tore his robe, shaved his head, and fell on the ground and worshiped. He said, 'Naked I came from my mother's womb, and naked shall I return there; the Lord gave, and the Lord has taken away; blessed be the name of the Lord.'

"In all this Job did not sin or charge God with wrong-doing" (1:20-21).

Further on, in replying to his wife he strongly reaffirms his acceptance even of the evil permitted by God. These verses are truly stupendous and we can never meditate on them enough. They emphasize the existence of pure love (which, however, will be put to the test throughout the Book, will be tested by fire a thousand times in his discourses with his friends), in the face of which there is the attitude of her from whom Job would have expected comfort and support.

We can recall that the ideal of comfort in trial is described in the Bible especially in the little Book of Ruth, when the Moabite woman stands at the side of Naomi, who is sorely tried, and does not abandon her. Naomi's husband, a Bethlehemite, had emigrated with his family because of a terrible famine that had broken out in Judea. After some time, he died and his two sons married Moabite women who did not belong to the chosen people. About ten years later the sons also died, and Naomi decided to return to her native land. She deeply loved her two daughters-in-law and advised each of them to return to their father's house, where they could begin a new life. One daughter accepted the advice, but Ruth did not want to go and said to Naomi: "Do not press me to leave you or to turn back from following you! Where you go, I will go; where you lodge, I will lodge; your people shall be my people, and your God my God. Where you die, I will die—there will I be buried. May the Lord do thus and so to me, and more as well, if even death parts me from you!" (Ruth 1:16-17).

These are the words that Job would have expected from his wife: if you are being tried, I am there with you, if you die, I will be with you; the Lord has tried you, let him try me also.

Instead the woman's response is cold: "Do you still persist in your integrity? Curse God and die." But he replies: "You speak as any foolish woman would speak" (2:9-10).

Not only does she not support her husband with encouragement, but she increases the temptation, provoking him to rebellion. So she herself succumbs to the trial because she does not understand the meaning of it.

The Causes of Misunderstandings *(meditatio)*

After having reread the biblical text, we now go on to reflect on it (as you see, it is a matter of exercising a method which in the future you can apply to the *lectio* of each page of Scripture).

Keeping in mind the brief observations we have made about the personages, and their more important actions and words, we want to ask ourselves: what is there in the wife's attitude that gives rise to misunderstanding? What kind of family problems appear because Job and his wife do not know how to bear the trial together? What teaching can we derive with regard to the problem of misunderstandings present even in the best families? For the family of Job is exceptional, he is a man of high moral stature, and we would never expect this strange relationship with his wife. Why do blocks in relationships occur even in family situations where there is faith, learning, formation, and spirituality?

We turn to our experience, sensitivity, and imagination, because the biblical passage offers us only a few words.

1. I think we can sense in the woman first of all a great *letdown:* the man in whom she believed, in whom she had placed all her trust, that man whom she saw so great, powerful, loved and esteemed, is now reduced to nothing. It is not simply a matter of egoism; the wife had invested much in her husband and now, aware that he no longer lives up to her expectations, she remains disillusioned, she feels almost betrayed. In fact—and here we encounter the mistaken interpretation of history, of the creature's relationship with God—since earlier Job was blessed by God, it follows that, if he has lost everything, then he has been abandoned by God.

Therefore there is a double disappointment: the husband has disappointed her in himself and before God. The heart of the woman is pierced by a terrible feeling of bitterness and solitude, because she no longer knows how and in whom to find support; this feeling turns into a vindictive outburst.

Together with the disillusionment there is *lack of trust:* the husband is no longer able to support her. The diabolical suspicion filters in; Satan had brought this suspicion into the presence of God, saying that perhaps Job was not honest and disinterested, that if he were devastated in his goods, he would close up in himself, unable to bear the situation. The woman shares this suspicion, she mistrusts her husband. She believes that his integrity depended on success and that when left with nothing, he can and will abandon his fidelity to God: "Curse God and die!" (We know that in the Bible this expression means: blaspheme, rebel, follow your destiny!)

Naturally her words are spoken out of exasperation and are not to be taken literally (many of the words Job will pronounce in the following poems express exasperation). Yet they indicate a decrease in trust, an inability to participate in the man's suffering, ignorance as to how to remain close to him. In substance the wife does not really understand her husband.

2. All this misunderstanding stems from a *mistaken judgment about God and Job.* She thinks that God has abandoned him when in reality God is testing him.

There are some other pages of the Bible which we can refer to in order to help us fill in the scarcity of available facts.

* First of all, an account from the Book of Kings in the cycle of the prophet Elisha. While Samaria is besieged, a terrible famine breaks out and the people, tried beyond their limit, ask the king's help, telling him that some women are even eating their children. Exasperated by the situation the king fears that the Lord has abandoned his people, and instead of joining the prophet Elisha in prayer, he decides to eliminate him: "So may God do to me, and more, if the head of Elisha son of Shaphat stays on his shoulders today" (2 Kings 6:31). The prophet must pay the penalty because he, in the name of God, has brought the people to ruin. The episode reaches its climax when the king sends a man ahead of him to the house of Elisha, who is seated with the elders. The prophet is aware that the king is coming to kill him and says to the elders: "'Are you aware that this murderer has sent someone to take off my head? When the messenger comes, see that you shut the door and hold it closed against him. Is not the sound of his master's feet behind him?' While he was still speaking with them, the king came down to him and said, 'This trouble is from the Lord! Why should I hope in the Lord any longer?' But Elisha said, 'Hear the word of the Lord: thus says the Lord, Tomorrow about this time a measure of choice meal shall be sold for a shekel, and two measures of barley for a shekel, at the gate of Samaria,'" that is, there will again be an abundance (2 Kings 6:32 - 7:1).

What happened? The king interpreted the siege and the famine as a curse from God and reacted with his own curse toward the prophet.

Likewise, Job's wife interpreted Job's misfortunes, as a curse of God and was upset with him, for in her eyes he was a man of God. Therefore she did not know how to help Job see the events as a trial, but suggested that he see everything as curse and punishment without escape. She did not understand her husband because she did not understand God.

The teaching for us is especially important: our misunderstandings are also a result of not understanding God deeply enough, of not contemplating him in his design of love and mercy, of becoming cold toward him.

* On this topic we find another interesting parallel in the Bible: the story of Tobit, a good and generous man, so generous that he gives up his meal in order to go and bury the dead at the risk of his own life. One day however he becomes blind. Why? Perhaps God has abandoned him?

In external matters his wife Anna is close to him and provides for the support of her husband. "At that time, also, my wife Anna earned money at women's work. She used to send what she made to the owners and they would pay wages to her" (Tobit 2:11-12).

Clearly she responds with courage and sacrifice to the situation of Tobit's blindness. However it happens that one day she receives from the owners a young goat as a sign of their satisfaction with her work. When he hears the bleat of the goat, Tobit becomes suspicious, thinks it has been stolen, does not believe the wife's explanation, and tells her to return the animal. Even more, he is flushed with shame for what Anna has done. At this point, the woman becomes angry and cries: "Where are your acts of charity? Where are your righteous deeds? These things are known about you" (cf. v 14). With his heart full of grief, Tobit weeps.

The fact that a quarrel breaks out between these two good persons, who love one another and love God, who willingly bear the trial and yet suffer internally, is significant. And they suffer badly, since Tobit in all probability thinks of himself as the great just one, the sufferer, while his wife is not on his level. Therefore he does not judge her justly and even believes her capable of a dishonest action. We should emphasize the fact that the serious error of suspecting his wife has its origin in his own honesty.

On her part Anna, aware of not being understood, gives vent to the bitterness that she has borne in her heart for a long time. She accuses her husband of non-existent faults, affirming that God is punishing both of them for Tobit's actions.

In reality the fault lies with both of them. These spouses had been close up to that moment; they had helped one another. However, they carried within some resentment which emerges in the face of trial, due to nervousness, fatigue, a wrong word.

Mutual resentment (thus, they did not understand one another in the deepest sense) and resentment toward God: God is punishing us, he no longer remembers us because of some wrongdoing on your or my part.

They have a mistaken, imperfect vision of God which can be present even in good and holy persons, and it wears down their relationship.

This is an initial idea to give direction to your meditation or reflection on the values of the text, so as to understand some problems that arise in every relationship between friends, in a group, and especially in the relationship of a couple, where the relations are more intimate and thus more delicate.

Suggestions Concerning Family Difficulties

Now we can ask ourselves what suggestions or indications concerning family difficulties can be found in the biblical pages on which we have reflected.

I will point out some very simple ones.

1. The first point is that these difficulties also touch persons who have achieved great inner purification. This comforts us, it urges us to remain humble and it allows us to understand many situations in which discord arises. We understand that on the one hand it is the Lord who tests us, and on the other there are negative realities which weigh on us and create the inability to help one another.

2. A second suggestion: trials, especially the most painful ones, are the litmus test of the couple's relationship. In fact, in them each is called to give the best of themselves, and by passing through very difficult sufferings and darkness each can achieve an extraordinary purification.

A while ago I was struck by the account of a Catholic journalist, who explained how he had lived through the last years with his wife who was sick with cancer. It was the wife who had perceived the importance of that trial and how they had to help one another bring to perfection, so to speak, their union as spouses. The journalist added that they had never spoken to one another, never understood one another as when they made that inexorable, implacable, devastating illness part of their relationship in order to live it together.

Trials are thus the litmus test and bring out the best in a person. Again the journalist remembered his wife's insistence on this point: that married persons have a different way even of dying, that is, they must learn to go through the experience of death together.

3. Difficulties stem not only from not understanding one another but also from not understanding well God and the meaning of suffering. When suffering is not put into focus in the presence of God, in prayer and faith, then mutual misunderstandings arise and latent resentment surfaces, because the person reaches the limits of his or her physical, psychological, moral and spiritual strength.

4. The last point is that when something goes wrong during these trials, the fault probably lies with both spouses. So it was in the case of Tobit and Anna who, however, overcome the trial, beginning from the husband's splendid prayer: "You are righteous, O Lord, and all your deeds are just; all your ways are mercy and truth; you judge the world. And now, O Lord, remember me and look favorably upon me. Do not punish me for my sins and for my unwitting offenses and those that my ancestors committed before you. They sinned against you, and disobeyed your commandments." He therefore recognizes his faults. And then he reads his story as the tragedy of a whole people; in fact he continues: "So you gave us over to plunder, exile and death, to become the talk, the byword, and an object of reproach among all the nations among whom you have dispersed us. And now your many judgments are true in exacting penalty from me for my sins" (Tobit 3:2-5).

Tobit not only overcomes the bitterness, the resentment, the sense of his own guilt, by placing his trust in

God the just judge, but he also succeeds in reading his personal suffering as a moment in the journey of humanity; a moment, we would say, in the trials of the Church, in the sufferings that each person has to bear. This seems to me an especially important point: even when trials are personal and touch us directly, they still concern the journey of the Church, the journey of humanity.

If we read them from this perspective, we can better perceive their meaning and find greater unity among us, because we become aware that they affect our relationship of joint responsibility toward family, society and the Church.

Jesus, the Church, the Trinity

In the moment of the *contemplatio* we are called to see beyond the pages we have read: Jesus, the Church, the Trinity, the mystery of God.

I will therefore seek to offer you some points for reflection, from which may arise the contemplation of the very mystery of God, a prolonged and affectionate prayer which nourishes us inwardly. For considerations are useful, they give direction to the mind, they excite the intelligence; however, from all this there must then pour forth contemplative, repeated prayer, in which one adores, praises, thanks, blesses, and exults. Our aridity, our dryness, our solitude are nourished especially by contemplation.

1. We may contemplate how the Church (and each one of us) always finds it difficult to remain near Jesus—humiliated, poor, crucified—just as the wife of Job is not able to be close to her husband during the trial.

We think, for example, of the difficulty Peter had, as clearly described in the Gospel according to Mark: "Then he began to teach them that the Son of Man must undergo great suffering, and be rejected by the elders, the chief priests, and the scribes, and be killed, and after three days rise again.... And Peter took him aside and began to rebuke him" (Mark 8:31-32), like the wife of Job, who invites him to rebel against God.

We think of the disciples in Gethsemane, who are not able to stand in the breach with Jesus but feel weighed down with weariness and fall asleep.

Thus the Church struggles to take part in the sufferings of Jesus, and in our personal struggle to share one another's sufferings we can read the very struggle of the Church.

Another example: today the western Church is suffering from the scarcity of priestly and religious vocations. Communities of women religious, especially, are experiencing moments of great affliction and suffering because of the aging of the members of the community, the lack of novices, and therefore the inability to carry on their works. And they ask themselves: Who is to blame? What have we done wrong? In reality this trial should be lived in faith, in intercession, in prayer, a prayer full of love and humility, full of peace. It is very wrong to want to wrest from God that which we want, thinking that it is due us and that the Lord does not listen because he is miserly in his gifts. It is very wrong to accuse one another, to want at any cost to discover the one who is responsible for a situation which should, on the contrary, help us grow in understanding, in mutual assistance, in mutual esteem, even within the sphere of the Church. We should live the scarcity of priestly and religious vocations by remaining close to the sufferings of Jesus, rather than fleeing from this difficulty and giving vent to bitterness, indignation and accusations.

2. Broadening the discourse, we could say that humanity finds it difficult to understand and accept the plan of God, the plan of salvation which passes through suffering and death. Instead of taking the side of Jesus it prefers to reject him and to depict for itself a fantastic future of pure success, pure power.

Let us then seek to live in our flesh the misunderstandings that exist in the Church and in humanity, purifying them in ourselves and in this way becoming intercessors. Let us remain in prayer before the crucified Christ together with Mary who was always united to the sufferings of Jesus.

For, what has been proposed to us in a negative way in the image of Job's wife or the wife of Tobit, is verified in a positive way in Mary, who knows how to remain close to her Son right to the end, sharing totally in his sufferings, without ever thinking that God has left him alone.

And when she hears Jesus exclaim: "My God, my God, why have you abandoned me?" she does not err in interpreting these words. She realizes that Jesus has reached the moment of a terrible trial of desolation and that she must therefore remain even closer to him.

Let us then enter into contemplation which, from reflection on our personal problems, will lead us to experience the very mystery of God.

Wholeheartedly Embrace
the Newness of the Gospel

(Homily on Saturday of the Twenty-fifth Week of Ordinary Time)

The first prayer of the liturgy has us ask for the grace to wholeheartedly embrace the newness of the Gospel.

This generic expression, "to wholeheartedly embrace the newness of the Gospel," must be specified more concretely for each one of us. It is thus important, especially during a spiritual retreat, to ask ourselves: what specific newness of the Gospel do I desire to re-embrace? What specific aspect of the newness of the Gospel does the Lord want us to re-embrace with his grace?

The two readings present us with a further reflection on the subject of the meditation: why and how do crises come? And why is it difficult to embrace the newness of the Gospel?

The Crises of Going Beyond

The prophet says: "I (Zechariah) looked up and saw a man with a measuring line in his hand. Then I asked, 'Where are you going?' He answered me, 'To measure Jerusalem, to see what is its width and what is its length.' Then the angel who talked with me came forward, and another angel came forward to meet him, and said to him, 'Run, say to that young man: Jerusalem shall be inhabited like villages without walls, because of the multitude of people and animals in it. For I will be a wall of fire all around it, says the Lord, and I will be the glory within it.'

"Sing and rejoice, O daughter Zion! For lo, I will come and dwell in your midst, says the Lord. Many nations shall join themselves to the Lord on that day, and shall be my people; and I will dwell in your midst. And you shall know that the Lord of hosts has sent me to you" (Zechariah 2:1-5, 10-11).

What is the message for us? The Old Testament passage teaches us that every crisis which seriously touches life is, like that of Job, a crisis of *going beyond*. It means passing from our manner of measuring God, others and ourselves, to a different manner, a broader one. This is the positive meaning even of the darkest, most sorrowful crises which can come about through misunderstanding, illness, the multiple ways of wearing down relationships.

All the crises which cause us to question ourselves are, seen from God's viewpoint, the place to make us go beyond, as is well expressed in the passage from the Book of Zechariah. One goes to measure the width and length of Jerusalem so as to be able to construct its walls. Within these walls the city will find its serenity, its prospects for happiness, its project. At the root of this intention there is a static, traditional, defensive vision of Jerusalem, of the Church, of the kingdom of God, and, for each one of us, of our plan for persons, family and society.

However, another angel comes unexpectedly and invites the angel accompanying the visionary to run to that young man and tell him that the measurements are useless because Jerusalem will not have walls; it should be open to welcome the multitude of people and animals. "I will be a wall of fire all around it, says the Lord, and I will be the glory within."

There is therefore a new project of which God is the promoter and guarantor. Crisis, fatigue, and suffering are experienced in the passage from a static, defensive vision to being open to the mystery of God who enlarges the confines of our lives.

Each time the Lord invites us, periodically in our existence, to broaden our horizons, even through dark moments whose meaning we don't understand, we enter upon the trial. But when we accept and welcome the divine economy for the world, society, the Church, the family, ourselves—in short, when we allow ourselves to be won over by the new plan of God, then joy springs forth: "Sing and rejoice, O daughter Zion! For lo, I will come and dwell in your midst, says the Lord. Many nations shall join themselves to the Lord on that day, and shall be my people."

In the page from Zechariah we perceive the seed of that new Jerusalem which will be described in the Book of Revelation, the new city in which there will no longer be the lamp, nor the light of the sun, because the Lord himself is the light.

However, while we contemplate the newness of this marvelous plan, we live the suffering and the drama of the passage from our measure to God's measure, we experience the crisis of not understanding the motive for that passage. The question that is orchestrated throughout the whole Book of Job is precisely this: why the trial? Why the darkness?

The Resistance of the Disciples

This same question emerges from the text of the Gospel of Luke, which shows the apostles' resistance to the broadening of their plan for Jesus.

"While everyone was amazed at all that he was doing, he said to his disciples, 'Let these words sink into your ears: The Son of Man is going to be betrayed into human hands.' But they did not understand this saying; its meaning was concealed from them, so that they could not perceive it. And they were afraid to ask him about this saying" (Lk 9:43-45).

Jesus lets them know the plan of the cross and of the glory, of the manifestation of the Father's love, of the revelation of the Trinity, which calls into question, at a deep level, the views of the disciples. They, in fact, resist so much that Luke emphasizes this resistance by repeating the same concept four times: "they did not understand," "its meaning was concealed from them," "they could not perceive it," "they were afraid to ask him about this saying."

They see neither the nature of nor the reason for the words of Jesus. They find his words obscure not only in themselves but even more in their meaning, in the broadening of the plan which the words give a presentiment of.

I think that the emotional block is well expressed, that block which often hinders us from understanding the new plans of God, and from questioning ourselves. When we are faced with an event that breaks into our life, we are so afraid of clashing with absurdity, we have so little trust in God that we prefer not to look within ourselves, and we do not even verbalize the fear we have within us.

Herein lies the root of many crises. The Lord asks us to overcome certain views, certain conditions of life, and we do not accept. Rather, the refusal is such that we don't even talk about it, we do not seek to question God or to question one another so as to understand that there must be a meaning. We shut ourselves up in immobility, in an interior suffering that chokes existence and paralyzes relationships.

Conclusion

As a summary of the teaching of God's Word we can say that crises come because there is need to go beyond, to enlarge our horizons, there is need for a new standard, a new measure of reality. If, however, this change is not accepted and we close ourselves off, we remain in solitude, suffering and darkness.

Let us think of the many families today who are thwarted by affective crises, crises of relationship, because persons do not even want to begin to listen to one another, to speak with one another, to question one another. Let us think of the enormous amount of suffering that this causes to humanity, and let us intercede for all these situations in the Church, in groups, in parishes, in couples and in families.

In the Eucharist let us unite our offering to that of Jesus Crucified, of his blood, of his passion, so that men and women, young and old, the healthy and the sick, may have the courage to believe that the Lord broadens the horizons of our life to the dimension of the heavenly Jerusalem. May they feel in their hearts the balm, the comfort, the serenity, the grace of the Holy Spirit.

And let us pray that the Lord, who in the Virgin Mary gave us the first fruits of creation, may enable each of us to daily embrace with our whole heart the newness of the Gospel.

In Dialogue with Families

(Practical instruction)

Before going on to the meditation on the family of Jacob, I would like to enter into a personal dialogue with you by offering a reply to the letters you have written to me to communicate your experience, so as to enrich the reflections which we have developed until now, and to offer some comments in reference to the Book of Job.

First of all, let us pray to the Lord for this day in which we live the resurrection of his Son Jesus.

"We entrust to you, Father, all those who, whether near or far, do not experience the joy of Sunday, who have difficulty in perceiving the power of the paschal mystery. We ask you to place each of us and our families under the power of the Spirit of the Risen One, so that we may witness that Jesus lives today in history, in peoples, in families. Grant that our faith be strong and fearless in the face of problems; that it be free, convinced, the fruit of interior decisions, and that we accept all the consequences it involves. May our faith be a communicator of peace and joy, may it be active in charity, in the desire to live at the service of our brothers and sisters, of the Church and of humanity. Grant us all this, Father, in union with Mary, through Christ our Lord. Amen."

The Message of Job and
the Journey of the *Equipe Notre Dame*

I quote from two letters which link the meditation on Job with the journey of the *Equipe Notre Dame*.

"In the case of Job and his wife, and in general in situations of misunderstanding among family members, there can be, underneath, a lack of harmony in communication, of a common growth in the faith. A positive reading stimulates us to make our own—even in happy family moments, in times of fullness—the words of Ruth: 'Wherever you go, I will go; wherever you die I will die also.' This union of faith can be attained through gaining awareness (*meditation*), prayer (*contemplation*), and concrete acts (*action*). In the method of the *Equipe Notre Dame* we speak of *conjugal prayer* and of the *duty to 'sit down together.'*

"It can happen in the life of a couple that one of the two spouses develops more, spiritually, than the other and this can be a source of misunderstanding. How can we smooth out such a situation? We are aware how precious is the means which the movement END offers us, which we call the *duty to sit down together*.

"It involves a monthly encounter between the spouses in the presence of God, for a conversation in which we are completely open with one another and together open with the Lord, so as to examine our life and our spiritual journey as a couple and a family. This method could be suggested to all couples united in the sacrament of Christian Marriage. Fidelity to this encounter, in fact, helps the couple's prayer as well as their ability to face, with the spirit of Job, any misunderstandings concerning the children, accepting the children as a gift of God and offering our crosses as the Father offered Christ."

I believe this experience of yours is very important and I think that the regular, punctual meeting of the couple can be a tremendous aid to understanding one another's individual spiritual journeys and to the mutual exchange of interior riches.

The "Heart" of Job

The following observation is also interesting: "Job communicates with his life (a blameless and upright man), he communicates with his words ('naked I came from my mother's womb, and naked shall I return there; the Lord gave, and the Lord has taken away; blessed be the name of the Lord'), but *where is his heart?* In the family, affective communication is fundamental."

Urged on by this question I reread the entire Book of Job. One truly has the impression that he is a blameless, upright man, however perhaps somewhat of an intellectual; a passionate person, certainly, but a passionate intellectual. Even his whole struggle with God is on the cutting edge of justice. In the end Job recognizes that he has been presumptuous, that he has not understood: "I had heard of you by the hearing of the ear, but now my eye sees you; and therefore I despise myself, and repent in dust and ashes" (42:5-6).

And so, in his first dispute we can read a certain presumption characteristic of one who is so upright, to one who does everything so well that he cannot understand the weaknesses of others and is severe toward them. We can find this attitude in ourselves also—because Job is a figure of the human person. When we have not received the mercy and love of God *with our whole heart* and do not feel attracted to God with all our feelings, with all our affection, we are rigid and harsh toward others who, in our judgment, do not act according to the law, the commandments.

I said that the observation is interesting because conjugal understanding, understanding in the family, must be drenched in mercy, in loving acceptance of the other who may not yet have attained that maturity of faith that I would wish for him or her.

The Inscrutable Designs of God

"Why does the Lord put his friends to the test? Why are the designs of God inscrutable, even if they are directed to our good? Is it part of an inscrutable mystery, the mystery of freedom, that Job does not succeed in converting his wife and does not have formative results with his children?"

The answer which Job gives at the end of the Book is that the designs are inscrutable precisely because they are *God's* designs, and therefore human beings understand them only by believing them, letting themselves be led, not demanding that they correspond to our justice. We, instead, want everything to be rational, reasonable. We do not accept the fact that God behaves in a mysterious manner, I would almost say in a more affective, more passionate manner, and at the same time a manner more suited to the complexity of our being. In the case of Job there is no explanation, but the story shows that in entrusting himself to God Job found his fullness, his family and himself. As long as he struggled, becoming exasperated with judgments he did not understand, he remained in his poverty.

Some paths for reflection open up which lie outside of the immediate scope of our retreat. I remember that some years ago I gave a course of Spiritual Exercises on Job. I myself was very impressed by his situation, which is always beyond our understanding, revealing to us that our mind can never completely grasp the problem, especially the problems of God. Only by accepting the fact of our limitations are we able to understand something, while if we rebel we remain absolutely in the dark.

Selflessness

"'Freely you have received, freely give.' What might be the obstacles to remove or the behavior and attitudes to activate so as to live our relationships selflessly? Paradoxically, at times it is more difficult to be agreeable with persons whom we love most; why? How can we live selflessly without the risk of feeling 'all powerful,' like heroes, losing the sense of humility? Sometimes we determine to 'love first,' but we do not persevere; why? And why are we unable to see unselfishness in the acts of our spouse? Again: often we do not succeed in being grateful to God who fills us with gifts we don't know how to recognize. Finally, how can we recognize the path that makes us grow in authentic selflessness without letting ourselves be stopped by the alibi of our limitations, by the real fear of pain and solitude?"

I would synthesize the questions of the letter this way: can Satan be right when he says that people do everything out of self-interest (let us recall the wager between God and Satan on man's ability to act unselfishly)?

Perhaps unselfishness appears to be very difficult, and it is; more difficult, perhaps, in daily situations than in great events. In fact, we often do not practice selflessness with those who are close to us, and we do not accept it.

I believe that profound selflessness is impossible to human beings, just as it is impossible for the rich man to enter the kingdom of heaven. As long as we are all basically somewhat rich, that is, jealous of what we have, of our autonomy, of knowing how to do things, selflessness as a constant attitude is impossible to us. Certainly, we live it on particular occasions, and yet not always and not in that manner which disposes us in humility to see reality as a gift of God, as a gift of the other, and not to take for granted the gifts that surround us.

However, unselfishness means having become fully children, having reached the perfection of the state of sonship, being, like the Son, in the Father and thus saying: Father, everything I have is from you, everything comes to me from you. This attitude constitutes an expropriation, a transparency, a loss of ourselves and of our autonomy. Therefore, even the journey of unselfishness is a gift to be sought continually from the Lord.

How, then, do we "recognize the path that makes us grow in authentic selflessness without letting ourselves be stopped by the alibi of our limitations, by real fear of pain and solitude?"

We can recognize it by contemplating Jesus and letting him wash our feet, so as to wash, in turn, the feet of our brothers and sisters. Conformation to Christ is the central point of Christian, filial existence. Opposed to it are any form of obstinacy or possessiveness, any attitude by which we take such full charge of ourselves as not to be able to understand how much we depend on others.

Selflessness, I said, is a gift to ask for even by means of the fatigue, suffering and humiliation we experience in living it so little.

So, in a certain sense, Satan is right: Job is not capable of real unselfishness, and he will be so only through a gift of God, which, however, he does not accept all at once. He has to pass through a great trial before freeing himself and realizing that he must not only give freely but also receive.

"The Culture of Living Together"

"When suffering comes from seeing our children choose a way of thinking and acting that is not only different from our plans but from that which we have always believed—and do believe—to be God's plan for the couple, then it is more difficult not to feel resentment and bitterness. How do we practice today *Job's respectful paternity?* The culture of living together, a kind of po-lygamy or polyandry, is more and more widespread, and perhaps presents problems similar to those of the African peoples. How can we not understand the diffi-dence of young people toward traditional matrimony, with the burden the woman has of the total responsibil-ity for daily life, with a social image that is static and closed? How can we propose striving toward the *total, mutual self-giving of man to woman and woman to man,* which we have believed and do believe is in the plan of God?"

Certainly, the statistics of the countries most ad-vanced in social and cultural development (North America, Canada, Northern Europe) show how the phe-nomenon called *individualism* (adult persons who make a life for themselves on their own) involves various types of temporary bonds. Herein lies the distrust of young people who are used to living by themselves and to binding themselves only temporarily, and who view tra-ditional marriage with suspicion, because it implies the totality of mutual gift and service.

How, then, "propose striving toward total mutual self-giving of man to woman and woman to man, as we have believed and do believe is in the plan of God?" In this question lies a central point for the future of Euro-pean society, a point which in 30 to 40 years will also be present in African and Asian societies, because technical progress drives us in the direction of making for our-selves a life that does not depend much on others. From this fact emerges the great *opportunity* for a total self-giving that is no longer necessarily forced by social cir-cumstances (at one time a man needed a wife, and a woman without a husband could not think of forming an existence for herself). Today everything becomes the ob-ject of free choice, of gift, of love, of unselfishness, of the most profound truth of the person.

Therefore, while on the one hand we must deplore the fact that society does not foster stability, on the other we must take the providential occasion for casting greater light on the truest being of man and woman, which is that of gift, of choice, not of constraint and social coercion.

The characteristic of *gift* in marriage appears stronger, whereas once the characteristics of social constraint and procreative service to society were dominant.

Obviously today this calls for greater maturity, and your mission in the Church consists in witnessing to the fact that the maturity of gift assists the human fulfillment of the person more than does social constraint. Certainly, we must always be attentive that the usages and customs of society do not lead to wrong-doing; however, we cannot turn them into obligations because society does not depend on us, we do not hold it in our hands.

The strength of the Gospel and of the humanizing Christian choice plays a formidable role. We must believe this without lingering to deplore the decadence of certain social bonds which made matrimony and its stability easier. Rather, we need to allow the affection, faith, mutual gift, and fidelity that form part of these bonds—as well as what Christ has been for human persons and for the Church—to emerge, without regret. These are the values which the condition of our society invites us to emphasize in a positive form.

Differences between Spouses in their Relationship with God

"The misunderstanding between Job and his wife arises from the difference between the spouses in their relationship with God. Job loves the Lord, while the wife loves the things given by the Lord to the point of rejecting God when these things are decreased. Even in families where learning, faith and spirituality are greater, there are misunderstandings if we forget that the couple must go to God and grow with him as a couple. For this reason the problem of spouses is to listen together to the Word of God."

The rejection of God when material goods are lacking lies at the center of not a few social dramas. When I lived in Rome, I had the opportunity to come to know and to visit the family of an ambassador to the Holy See. I was very shocked to learn, a few years later, that, not having gone any higher in his career, that ambassador committed suicide after having killed his wife. He had reached the point of committing this tragic act because the wife continually reproved him for his lack of success, since he did not obtain for his family the abundance of material things she had hoped for.

The news of the double death was a real *shock* for me because I had had the occasion for appreciating that man's sensitivity, refinement of soul, and ability to listen.

This example signifies that attachment to riches and glory is always a danger and distorts our relationship with God. When we possess goods, we must manage them in poverty of spirit and with the awareness of our weakness as creatures. Listening to the Word of God, when it is experienced by both spouses together, is undoubtedly an aid to growing together in the faith.

However, I ask myself this question: is it really a bad thing for the relationship of each spouse with God to differ? Certainly they should strive for a common relationship; however, the Bible shows us that the ways of relating to God are never identical. Experience teaches in particular that the woman relates to God in a different way than does the man. I am convinced that such diversity should be respected, in fact, that it should be increased. Couples need to respect one another, encourage one another, while allowing each spouse to have a secret space in his or her journey to God. The good effects of this will be felt, without pretending to reduce them to a logical and precise analysis. It does not seem right to me that the woman should want to understand everything about the man, or vice versa, because we can never understand everything about the mystery of a person's relationship with God.

Diversity of Histories

"If the harmony of the couple is problematic due to either a different spiritual preparation or, more often, to differences in character, habit, education, etc., how do we find a remedy? It seems to me that problems of a psychological nature have a real effect on married life and a couple's good will can compensate only so far. I know couples who want to carry out a spiritual journey and yet experience obstacles in understanding and lack of dialogue, or they dialogue on superficial topics, because to go deeper would increase disagreements and misunderstandings. What can we do?"

This is a fundamental question: can differences truly be reconciled?

Obviously your experience can offer better responses than mine. However, I believe that many differences between spouses necessarily remain, that diversity is to be accepted as part of the relationship, not only when it is enriching but also when it is painful and thus causes a problem because, for example, a couple does not succeed in dialoguing about serious and deep topics without disagreements and misunderstanding.

We must accept diversity before overcoming it, out of respect for the other, out of love for the other and for the mystery of God. Diversity is part of the human journey. One who forms an idyllic vision in which it will one day be possible to overcome all differences, is dreaming of an earthly paradise.

On the other hand, the very experience of the visible Church, of the historical Church, is that of diversity, of understanding that is not complete. Even the lives of the saints are marked by this kind of conflict. In this century we have witnessed the canonization of Pius X and the beatification of Andrea Carlo Cardinal Ferrari. These two pastors should have enjoyed a deep mutual understanding because they were both committed to ecclesiastical service. Yet they did not understand one another well and had some notable disagreements. Who was at fault? Perhaps both of them, but it is a fact that they suffered very much over this mutual misunderstanding.

Therefore, our problems in understanding one another do not stem from the fact that we are not saints. Holiness does not eliminate differences and misunderstandings, but is first of all able to humbly accept them. It is also necessary to accept not knowing whom to blame for disagreements. This attitude is more constructive than one that wants to resolve everything at all costs or that pretends to find in psychology the way to solve the problem.

With acceptance and humility some steps can be made, some actions can be taken, dialogue can be somewhat deepened.

The journey of small steps, to be studied daily and made with joy, is more modest but more realistic than global ideals. The latter are always to be kept in view, because we will realize them in eternal life. But if they are translated too quickly into daily reality they end up disappointing us.

I leave it to you to reread the numerous pages of Scripture on this topic. I limit myself to recalling the disagreement between Paul and Barnabas with regard to Mark. They did not understand one another, they argued, and they separated, each going his own way. Yet they were two holy men who had worked together for years in perfect agreement.

Poverty

Broadening the theme of the relationship of the couple as selfless gift to one another, one letter emphasizes the importance of poverty.

"In going to the source of the crises, we note a formative lack precisely in the area of the spouses' relationship, not only from the viewpoint of sexuality but especially from the viewpoint of the real essence of the couple's relationship, which is 'a free gift of self' to the other.

"We educate our children to obtain—in search of their own satisfaction—the maximum material well-being with the minimum output of energy. We give them criteria for evaluation which are of this world, not of God.

"The couple, the family, the Church, must follow the way of *economic poverty* (not just spiritual), because it is the way capable of bringing us to a real welcoming and acceptance of God's providence. Catechesis and pastoral initiatives should spur us on to the promotion, the development, the journey and the permanent verification of a life lived responsibly in Christian poverty."

Poverty is a basic condition for the Church and its initiatives. We all understand that it is a difficult point that is never resolved and about which we must make a discernment every day. In fact, in a sense, the poverty of the hermit who withdraws into the desert is much easier (and he might even boast about his radical choice and become proud, as often happened to hermits in the past).

Instead, those who live in the midst of the contradictions of a troubled world and have responsibilities toward others in the family, in the parish, in society, in the Church, must accept the administration of goods and an economic system concretely geared to the market, and seek to imbue it with the spirit of evangelical poverty. This poverty in the use of things is very problematic because no manual offers us the formula.

How right is it for the Church to have material goods or to dispose of them? In disposing of them, to what extent does it act according to the Gospel? To what extent, instead, does it let itself be swayed by the spirit of the world? Only through listening to the Word of God and through prayer can we make choices that are in accord with the heart of Christ.

One of my daily sufferings results from asking myself: will this specific choice, which might even be criticized today because it seems to be counter to the spirit of poverty, be considered right ten or twenty years from now, or not? For example, when Paul VI wanted the construction of Nervi Hall, he was overwhelmed by criticism from those who thought it was unnecessary. Today, some years later, the people who gather in that hall understand its importance because it gives about ten thousand people the possibility of communicating with the Pope.

The dilemma of poverty is unending: on the one hand we need more houses; however houses without churches risk becoming places of bitterness and solitude. On the other hand, churches without houses are deserted, they are of no use. Those who accept being part of the complexity of life must also accept the fact of not always knowing whether their choice is right, must accept the need to question themselves, the risk of being criticized. They must do what seems best to them and leave the judgment to history.

This is also valid for families: we need to dispose of a certain amount of possessions, but with the generosity of Abraham or Jacob and with the poverty and humility of Jesus.

On this point it is dangerous to let oneself be influenced by ideologies. Consumerism is an ideology, just as pauperism is, because every choice that leads to excess becomes ideological. In the history of the Church there have been numerous battles, innumerable disagreements over poverty. This signifies that the everyday good sense of the idea is more important, a good sense which, in confronting itself with the Gospel, chooses day after day whatever is right and opportune.

We cannot then have an a priori precise standard, a codified remedy. Our standard is the contemplation of the poor and humble Jesus. Then we let ourselves be guided by the Holy Spirit, with the willingness to be corrected if we have erred. To me it seems that this way is more sanctifying than that of the hermit in the desert. Apart from the fact that if, at a certain point, the hermit is joined by many disciples and brothers, then the question of building houses, of having farms to cultivate the land from which their bread comes, of buying medicine for the sick, etc., surfaces again. Certain monastic complexes arising from a hermit's way of life, clearly show that while beginning from an initial form of absolute, radical poverty, they could not avoid some costly structures which, in the end, no longer corresponded to the original ideal.

I believe that the Word of God, in becoming incarnate, was aware of all these situations and therefore knew he was setting in motion an ambiguous process. However, he loves us to the point of accepting the fact that there would be ambiguities in history, and he gives us the humility to correct them.

Conclusion

Your letters have given rise to many reflections which I entrust to each one of your families, that you may take them up again and verify them in your daily commitment. It would be useful to look for other biblical passages which shed light on the themes we have just touched on, and meditate on them in an atmosphere of silence, prayer and even dialogue.

"We offer you, O Lord, all the harshness and difficulties of the journey. Grant that we, through a leap in the quality of our faith, may succeed in perceiving how you are at work, and how Jesus Christ is unifying families and humanity; how trials, suffering and pain can become paths toward unity, toward communion, in the grace of Jesus who, on the cross, with Mary near him, offers his life for all men and women on earth. Amen."

Reconciling Differences

"Lord Jesus, you were not afraid to place at the root of your existence among us and of your work, families, tribes and peoples that were greatly divided. You were not afraid to enter into a humanity that was unreconciled and at variance. Grant that, through a humble reflection on our divisions, on our disagreements, even small and simple ones, we may grasp the mystery of the great reconciliation which you accomplish on the cross, which you continue to accomplish through the Church and the Eucharist. Grant that we ourselves may become, through your grace, instruments of reconciliation and peace. You who live and reign with the Father in the unity of the Holy Spirit, forever and ever. Amen."

This second meditation is more complex than the first because it concerns a long story, the longest in the Bible. In fact, it unfolds through the course of many chapters, from 37 to 50 of the Book of Genesis. It is the story of Joseph, son of Jacob, and his brothers. We read, in fact, in verse 2 of chapter 37: "This is the story of the family of Jacob," of the sons of this great patriarch to whom God himself gave the name *Israel* which would become the name of the people of God.

The whole account is concerned with the relationship between father, sons and brothers. It is fascinating, dramatic, rich in instruction. Humanity with its passions, problems, and relationships, whether family, social or political, emerges strongly in it. This account is called *secular* because, in fact, it speaks little of God; it is as though the divine were inserted in daily life.

I advise you to take your time to read all these chapters of Genesis during the next few months, because they contain a marvelous and particularly instructive narrative. I will simply indicate the characteristics which refer to the struggle to reconcile differences, offering you the meditation in a rather embryonic manner, giving you some starting points to be deepened in the verification of your experience as family. In reality, the story presents us with a very troubled family, and it describes a journey of ruptures, divisions and then reconciliation. A family in which the relationships are very intricate; therefore the story helps us to understand that even the most desperate situations can be resolved. We actually read about the attempt to kill one of the brothers, and the whole event is a theater of differences which do not succeed in getting along together. For this reason, notwithstanding its harshness, it is interesting.

I will indicate some points for the *lectio* of chapter 37 and for the *meditatio* of chapters 39 to 50 of Genesis.

Genesis 37

"Joseph, being seventeen years old, was shepherding the flock with his brothers; he was a helper to the sons of Bilhah and Zilpah, his father's wives; and Joseph brought a bad report of them to their father. Now Israel loved Joseph more than any other of his children, because he was the son of his old age; and he had made him a long robe with sleeves. But when his brothers saw that their father loved him more than all his brothers, they hated him, and could not speak peaceably to him.

"Once Joseph had a dream, and when he told it to his brothers, they hated him even more. He said to them, 'Listen to this dream that I dreamed. There we were, binding sheaves in the field. Suddenly my sheaf rose and stood upright; then your sheaves gathered around it, and bowed down to my sheaf.' His brothers said to him, 'Are you indeed going to reign over us? Are you indeed to have dominion over us?' So they hated him even more because of his dream and his words.

"He had another dream, and told it to his brothers, saying, 'Look, I have had another dream: the sun, the moon, and eleven stars were bowing down to me.' But when he told it to his father and to his brothers, his father rebuked him, and said to him, 'What kind of dream is this that you have had? Shall we indeed come, I and your mother and your brothers, and bow to the ground before you?' So his brothers were jealous of him, but his father kept the matter in mind.

"Now his brothers went to pasture their father's flock near Shechem. And Israel said to Joseph, 'Are not your brothers pasturing the flock at Shechem? Come, I will send you to them.' He answered, 'Here I am.' So he said to him, 'Go now, see if it is well with your brothers and with the flock; and bring word back to me.' So he sent him from the valley of Hebron.

"He came to Shechem, and a man found him wandering in the fields; the man asked him, 'What are you seeking?' 'I am seeking my brothers,' he said; 'tell me, please, where they are pasturing the flock.' The man said, 'They have gone away, for I heard them say, "Let us go to Dothan."' So Joseph went after his brothers, and found them at Dothan. They saw him from a distance, and before he came near to them, they conspired to kill him. They said to one another, 'Here comes this dreamer. Come now, let us kill him and throw him into one of the pits; then we shall say that a wild animal has devoured him, and we shall see what will become of his dreams.' But when Reuben heard it, he delivered him out of their hands, saying, 'Let us not take his life.' Reuben said to them, 'Shed no blood; throw him into this pit here in the wilderness, but lay no hand on him'—that he might rescue him out of their hand and restore him to his father. So when Joseph came to his brothers, they stripped him of his robe, the long robe with sleeves that he wore; and they took him and threw him into a pit. The pit was empty; there was no water in it.

"Then they sat down to eat; and looking up they saw a caravan of Ishmaelites coming from Gilead, with their camels carrying gum, balm, and resin, on their way to carry it down to Egypt. Then Judah said to his brothers, 'What profit is it if we kill our brother and conceal his blood? Come, let us sell him to the Ishmaelites, and not lay our hands on him, for he is our brother, our own flesh.' And his brothers agreed. When some Midianite traders passed by, they drew Joseph up, lifting him out of the pit, and sold him to the Ishmaelites for twenty pieces of silver. And they took Joseph to Egypt.

"When Reuben returned to the pit and saw that Joseph was not in the pit, he tore his clothes. He returned to his brothers, and said, 'The boy is gone; and I, where can I turn?' Then they took Joseph's robe, slaughtered a goat, and dipped the robe in the blood. They had the long robe with sleeves taken to their father, and they said, 'This we have found; see now whether it is your son's robe or not.' He recognized it, and said, 'It is my son's robe! A wild animal has devoured him; Joseph is without doubt torn to pieces.' Then Jacob tore his garments, and put sackcloth on his loins, and mourned for his son many days. All his sons and all his daughters sought to comfort him; but he refused to be comforted, and said, 'No, I shall go down to Sheol to my son, mourning.' Thus his father bewailed him. Meanwhile the Midianites had sold him in Egypt to Potiphar, one of Pharoah's officials, the captain of the guard."

We are not concerned with the precise exegesis of the passage and neither will we pause to consider the different traditions and sources which appear clearly enough in the account. For example, vv. 3 and 10 speak of Rachel as still alive and Benjamin not yet born, while according to chapter 35, the mother is already dead and thus Benjamin, in chapter 37, is already born. Likewise, in verses 12-36 it is not clear whether it is Reuben or Judah who saves Joseph from death, and whether it is the Ishmaelites or the Midianites who lift him out of the cistern and sell him in Egypt.

The Personages

Who are the principal personages in chapter 37?

1. The first is *Joseph*. He was young (seventeen years old), handsome, and he would certainly have attracted the attention of the young women, and of the people in general. The emphasis on the sons of Bilhah and Zilpah shows at once that we are faced with a complex family situation: Jacob is a polygamist. He has two wives who are called free or of the first degree—Leah and Rachel—for whom he worked several years in Mesopotamia; then he has two other wives who are slaves. The twelve sons are the fruit of these relationships, and a cause of tension between the wives. It is a tangle symbolic of the condition of humankind and also of the chosen people, of Israel, born from these tribes which feel the effects of the father's compromises and carry within them the seed of all successive sufferings.

2. After Joseph there are *the brothers*, who are referred to in general (because they were already named one by one in chapter 35:23-26) where it says: "Joseph brought a bad report of them to their father." They are not exemplary, and the Bible tells us of some of their

exploits. For example, chapter 38 is dedicated to the dramatic but at the same time humorous story of Judah and Tamar, which was handed down since they are part of the genealogy of Jesus.

3. *The father:* "Israel loved Joseph more than any other of his children, because he was the son of his old age; and he had made him a long robe with sleeves" (v. 3).

With this mention of the father the root of the problem emerges, that is, inequality: he loves that son more than all the others and actually weaves him a tunic with long sleeves, which is the clothing of a king. It is easy to imagine the gossip this gesture aroused: so we have to work while Joseph doesn't? He is a gentleman and who are we? Forms of resentment to which Jacob is blind.

The mother is missing from among the personages, and probably the whole story is so dramatic precisely for this reason. She is not there to open the eyes of her husband, to smooth out hostilities, to persuade Joseph not to recount his dreams. Historically she is not there because she has died; oddly enough, Jacob invokes her ("Shall we indeed come, I and your mother and your brothers, and bow to the ground before you?"); however, her active presence is lacking.

It is not too hazardous a parallel to recall that even at Cana the event would have had a sad outcome without the intervention of Mary.

The Destructive Elements Within the Family

Let us now try to point out the *destructive elements* which are breaking up the family.

* One is the *inequality* which the elderly father somewhat foolishly creates. We read, in fact: "But when his brothers saw that their father loved him more than all his brothers, they hated him and could not speak peaceably to him" (v. 4). However, it is not so much Joseph who is not accepted on account of the distinction, but

Jacob. Joseph is hated because his father loves him so much. It is the action of the father which provokes the brothers who, while they preserve a sense of reverence toward Jacob, pour out their anger on the defenseless young man.

* Another element which brings about the destruction of relationships is a kind of *foolishness*, perhaps not culpable, on Joseph's part: the innocent recounting of his dreams. He hadn't the least idea that he aroused *envy and rancor* in the others: "Once Joseph had a dream, and when he told it to his brothers, they hated him even more" (v. 5).

So the father makes a mistake, the brothers behave badly, but even Joseph does not realize how difficult it is to live balanced family relationships, how necessary it is to respect the feelings of others.

* Little by little, the misunderstandings and the resentment lead to the drama which probably no one wanted, and yet it happens: *the plan of the crime* ("they conspired to kill him"). First the brothers had not thought of it, even though they detested Joseph. Certainly, if some accident had befallen him, they would have been content, they would not have wept, but the idea of killing him was still far from their minds. However, in a moment of folly, of exaltation, even due to too much wine, they see him arrive from a distance, wearing his robe with the long sleeves, and they agree to do away with him.

The long description is interesting. And we note that, while Reuben (the firstborn of Leah) and Judah (also a son of Leah) agreed to punish him so as then to rescue him or to sell him into slavery, all the brothers are guilty of betraying the young Joseph.

* The last of these destructive actions is the *lie*.

After having betrayed and sold him, "they took Joseph's robe, slaughtered a goat, and dipped the robe in the blood. They had the long robe with sleeves taken to their father, and they said, 'This we have found; see now whether it is your son's robe or not.' He recognized it, and said, 'It is my son's robe! A wild animal has devoured him; Joseph is without doubt torn to pieces.' Then Jacob tore his garments, and put sackcloth on his loins, and mourned for his son many days. All his sons and all his daughters sought to comfort him; but he refused to be comforted, and said, 'No, I shall go down to Sheol to my son, mourning.' Thus his father bewailed him" (vv. 31-35).

To their hatred against their brother they add the insult to their father, wanting to toy cruelly with his feelings, making him believe that a ferocious animal had devoured Joseph. And there is the lie, because when the brothers see their father cry, they pretend to be moved and weep with him.

This falsehood becomes permanent and accompanies them for years. We can imagine the life of this family in which each one fears that someday one of them will tell the truth. It is a kind of *conspiracy* of silence which holds all of them subject in guilt, each one distrustful and full of fear.

Through a perverse mechanism, an incurable division has been introduced into the circle of a great family which later becomes Israel, then the people of God, the beginning of the Church, the chosen people in its initial formation.

This dramatic event concerns the very mystery of humanity, and it is worthwhile to deepen our understanding of it in personal reflection, not only from the literary or emotional or psychological viewpoint, but from a theological one. We are this family.

The conspiracy of silence, the plot against the father, would have weighed upon Jacob's family forever if there had not been the reconciling action of God. This means that God can reconcile the most desperate situations, those which seem frozen in lies and perverseness. As we shall see, Joseph and his brothers will be led by a series of providential actions in which each will rediscover his truth and achieve reconciliation: Joseph with his brothers, the brothers with their father, the father with his sons, all together with the memory of their mother. We can thus read in the account the story of the instruments through which God reconciles.

I believe it's useful to help ourselves with an example. You know better than I how resentment toward the father, the inability to accept him, the desire to be different from him, is a phenomenon present in many families. It can sometimes explain the reason for cyclic changes, which at first appear strange. I know some families in which the father is an atheist and, by contrast, a son or daughter chooses the religious life or priesthood; later there is the cycle of the grandchildren who abandon the faith. When, wrongly or rightly, there are motives of non-acceptance, there is a fatal clash. But the Lord, from on high, sees and keeps watch. We look at the dramatic aspect of it because we have in mind only a moment of the cycle. And so we rejoice when there is a vocation in the family of the atheist, and suffer when atheism arises from a believing family. But the Lord knows how to bring everyone home. He knows, as did Jacob who in the evening offered sacrifices for his sons, yet he doesn't remove the anxiety or joy in the different situations.

From this long biblical story, perennial family problems come to light which enable us, if not to explain everything, at least to better penetrate the complexity of reality.

And we must pray for all humanity afflicted by divisions and by unreconciled differences, in the certainty that God takes care of them and calls us, as

Church, to take care of them together with him.

The Actors in the Reconciliation

Chapters 39 to 50 of Genesis recount to us the long reconciling action of Joseph to overcome the different kinds of division and opposition within his family.

They are very beautiful pages, which show how much wisdom, patience and amiability is employed to restore unity to this tangle of hatred, blood, lies and cruelty. Truly extraordinary pages which emphasize how divided humanity is called to reconciliation.

Who takes part in this reconciliation? There are four: God, Joseph, the brothers, and the father. The story picks up again with the instruments of the division, by means of a backward journey which requires effort, because wounds of the heart need time to heal. This is true even at the level of society: the wounds produced by terrorism (to give an example close to us) take many years to heal. Even if it were desirable, it is hard to hasten certain times, and the Scriptures take account of the psychological factors. We cannot accomplish hurriedly whatever calls for long maturation; we need to prepare ourselves to have much patience.

1. The first actor is *God* who, however, hardly ever appears. In the story of Joseph there is no miraculous intervention, there are no prophecies. Yes, there are dreams, but they are not decisive. God leads us to reconciliation, as we have noted, through the movements of ordinary providence.

It is by providential circumstance that Joseph makes his fortune in Egypt. It is not extraordinary that a famine comes and the people in Canaan travel to Egypt to obtain bread. God, who is always at work in reconciliation, often hides himself in the ordinary and so-called providential events of life; it is up to us to distinguish and recognize them.

2. God uses instruments. First of all *Joseph,* who was rejected by his brothers as a sign of division, as the beloved one of the father, and was hated for this. By divine disposition he becomes the instrument for the reconciliation of the whole family. Naturally Joseph himself has to accomplish a journey. He needs to be purified of his childish dreams, which he recounts with too much self-confidence. He needs to show more understanding toward his brothers, to learn to put himself in their shoes. Since he was born of Rachel, the beloved wife of Jacob, it always seemed obvious to him that he was the favorite, and he did not think of the others.

The terrible events he will pass through—finding himself in the cistern, being sold as a slave, being repaid with imprisonment for his fidelity to Potiphar—gradually purify him, teaching him to understand the complex nature of situations, to understand that we cannot always have what we want in life (as children believe), that success involves severe discipline. Joseph learns the lesson at a high price and becomes a wise and upright man, able to recognize God's plan in history and so to reconcile his brothers.

Two texts in particular shed light on this topic: Genesis 45:2-5 and 50:19-21.

* Joseph is appointed viceroy of Egypt because he knows how to interpret Pharaoh's dreams. He suggests gathering the surplus of the good years to provide for the great famine. When the famine strikes the earth, the sons of Jacob also journey from Canaan to Egypt to purchase grain. They meet their brother who, without letting them recognize him, gives them what they need. First, however, he places them in trouble, he tries them, and the brothers begin to feel remorse for their past sin, they believe God is punishing them. Finally Joseph sends them home, making them promise to return with Benjamin.

When the second meeting takes place, Joseph has a mysterious banquet prepared, then orders the servants to fill the sacks of the brothers with grain and money, and to place a silver cup in Benjamin's sack. The next morning, just as the brothers are leaving the city, they are approached by the court steward who accuses them of theft and threatens to imprison the one whose sack contains the cup. It is a very hard trial for Jacob's sons. Judah intervenes, as we shall see, and so in chapter 45, Joseph reveals himself: "And he wept so loudly that the Egyptians heard it, and the household of Pharaoh heard it. Joseph said to his brothers, 'I am Joseph. Is my father still alive?' But his brothers could not answer him, so dismayed were they at his presence. Then Joseph said to his brothers, 'Come closer to me.' And they came closer. He said, 'I am your brother, Joseph, whom you sold into Egypt. And now do not be distressed, or angry with yourselves, because you sold me here; *for God sent me before you to preserve life'*" (Genesis 45:2-5).

This is the salvific reading of the story; everything that happened and caused so much suffering to Joseph was for the salvation and the future of the people of God. Of course, if Joseph had thought only of himself, he probably would have taken revenge. Instead he perceives that he is part of a divine plan for the salvation of a people and so acquires an extraordinary ability to reconcile.

In addition, the account is very long because it is not narrated that Joseph reveals himself to his brothers and makes everything right by saying that now there is peace. Instead, he initiates a gradual and progressive process to arouse good sentiments in his brothers, so that they confess their sin and repent.

In fact, when persons have been altered by criminal and unjust actions, it is not enough to tell them: 'now go in peace'; we must help such persons to recognize their errors and to change.

Joseph is naturally involved in this long and difficult journey, he is moved, he gives vent to his sufferings, he breaks into tears; however, he resists, he is patient, so as to achieve a real, profound reconciliation, one that is not simply sentimental. This is expressed in the passage of chapter 45, which we have quoted.

* Genesis 50:19-21. Jacob has died and the brothers fear they will be punished by Joseph, so they send a message asking him to pardon them according to the wish expressed by their aged father. Then they go to him in person, throwing themselves on the ground. However, the words they hear indicate once more the wisdom of their brother and his broad understanding of the salvific plan of God: "Do not be afraid! Am I in the place of God? Even though you intended to do harm to me, God intended it for good, in order to preserve a numerous people, as he is doing today. So have no fear; I myself will provide for you and your little ones."

3. The *brothers* themselves are actors in the reconciling process, even if more passive. I have already alluded to the moment in which they fear that God is punishing them for having betrayed the boy Joseph. The best sentiments, however, are expressed in the speech of Judah, one of the most beautiful in the whole Bible, one of the most moving and best constructed orations, from a literary viewpoint. He addresses his brother, saying: "O my lord, let your servant please speak a word in my lord's ears, and do not be angry with your servant; for you are like Pharaoh himself. My lord asked his servants, saying, 'Have you a father or a brother?' And we said to my lord, 'We have a father, an old man, and a younger brother, the child of his old age. His brother is dead; he alone is left of his mother's children, and his father loves him.'

Then you said to your servants, 'Bring him down to me, so that I may set eyes on him.' We said to my lord, 'The boy cannot leave his father, for if he should leave his father, his father would die.' Then you said to your servants, 'Unless your youngest brother comes down with you, you shall see my face no more.' When we went back to your servant my father we told him the words of my lord. And when our father said, 'Go again, buy us a little food,' we said, 'We cannot go down. Only if our youngest brother goes with us, will we go down; for we cannot see the man's face unless our youngest brother is with us.' Then your servant my father said to us, 'You know that my wife bore me two sons; one left me, and I said, "Surely he has been torn to pieces; and I have never seen him since. If you take this one also from me, and harm comes to him, you will bring down my gray hairs in sorrow to Sheol."' Now therefore, when I come to your servant my father and the boy is not with us, then, as his life is bound up in the boy's life, when he sees that the boy is not with us, he will die; and your servants will bring down the gray hairs of your servant our father with sorrow to Sheol. For your servant became surety for the boy to my father, saying, 'If I do not bring him back to you, then I will bear the blame in the sight of my father all my life.' Now therefore, please let your servant remain as a slave to my lord in place of the boy; and let the boy go back with his brothers. For how can I go back to my father if the boy is not with me? I fear to see the suffering that would come upon my father" (Genesis 44:18-34). Immediately after this the recognition takes place.

Then Judah, one of those who had formulated the plot, even though in a more moderate form, asks for mercy and speaks with love of himself, his father, and his brothers. He has regained his affection for his father and for Benjamin, the favorite of his father as Joseph had been before him (he thus also regained his affection for Joseph). He has become aware of family unity, of their being twelve brothers (already in Genesis 42:13, the brothers had told Joseph they were "twelve"); he has re-expressed their fraternal communion.

4. Throughout the story the *elderly father* is present, who at the beginning had been somewhat guilty of partiality. In the end he allows himself to be brought to Egypt to be reunited with his family, won over by the love of those sons who had lied to him.

It will not be difficult to draw the message for today from this splendid and psychologically rich account of reconciliation, to understand which are the conditions, the modes, the instruments, the efforts necessary to bring about reconciliation in families, in the Church, and in society.

The Contemplation of the Plan of God

For the *contemplatio*, I invite you to go beyond the story of Joseph and his brothers, to consider the plan of God.

* Joseph, in fact, is a figure of the people of Israel and the brothers are a figure of the Nations that cannot accept the fact of a privileged Israel; it is the drama of universal history.

The election of Israel is not a wrong done to other peoples, it is not to be experienced as an injustice toward those who are not Hebrew. We must learn to contemplate the passion of love of God, who creates a history of salvation. As long as we don't understand, we will be always be menaced by divisions and wars.

* Joseph is also a figure of Jesus, of the Church, and the brothers are a figure of humankind. Just as he does not accept Israel, so the rationalistic and "enlightened" man is not able to accept a Church which has some privileges of salvation: why do we need to become

Christian? Why is salvation only in Jesus Christ? Here, in comparison among religions, arise the obstacles to interfaith dialogue. Christians themselves sometimes live their faith with anxiety: why should we be the only religion of salvation?

Here we are bound to a vision based on pure reason: there is no history of love, no divine plan of salvation for everyone which makes use of privileged instruments; we are all alike. We do not want inequalities in the human historical journey, we do not accept divisions in humanity, and at times we suffer very much because of this. We do not succeed in reconciling our modern or post-modern mentality with the fact of our being Christians. It is therefore extremely important, with the grace of the Holy Spirit, to attain what we have seen to be the fundamental intuition of the whole story of Joseph: "God sent me before you to preserve life" (45:5).

The privilege of Israel with respect to other nations, the privilege of Jesus with respect to other men, and the privilege of the Church, is for the salvation of all, as is clearly seen in the crucified Son. The privilege of Jesus is given him that he might die for all; the privilege of the Church is given it that it might serve humanity and that, by means of this service and gift of life, humanity might be one. Thus, humanity is not unified simply by means of a collection of equals, but by Jesus who, in offering his life as the firstborn, calls and draws us all to himself.

It is not an easy vision; in fact, it demands acceptance of a plan of God which does not correspond to a purely evolutionary development, as is postulated by reason, identical for everyone, in which salvation lacks an historical dimension (according to an idealistic, gnostic vision). Instead it concerns the love of God who has created the world with a plan of salvation which has its fulfillment in Jesus Christ.

Today we witness the struggle between these two

conceptions: for one, the dignity of the person is founded on pure rationality; for the other, it is founded on the universal attraction which Jesus exercises over everyone. Joseph is a figure of the just one sacrificed for others, the one who in the end is recognized as the unique instrument of salvation. The only way humanity has been saved from hunger has been through this rejected Jesus.

We must ask the Lord to make us understand and love the mystery of the story of Joseph, and to enable us to make this mystery loved. It is the mystery that will save humankind from spiritual malnutrition, from death through spiritual hunger. There is no reason, no law, no international structure, however perfect, that can save humanity; only the redemption.

* Joseph is also a figure of the mission some individuals may have in families and some families may have for others.

We are not alike even in the Church; there are certain missions raised up by the Lord. A family may be saved by only one member of that family, and some families may save others.

The acceptance of service by some for others is part of the mystery of election, of the mystery of salvation which is diffused not by sprinkling but rather from a fountain from which all can draw.

It is the invitation to accept the differences not only in the Church and in history, but in our own families.

Certainly it is a beautiful thing if the family is united in the mystery of God to the point that there are almost no differences between members. However, many families will be saved by one member (the father, the mother, the child or relative). Apart from the divisions caused by our nature marked by sin, there is a divine variety which appears right from the moment of creation, in which one reality is linked to the others in service. Light, sun are at the service of life on earth;

vegetable life is at the service of animal life; animal life is at the service of human beings, who in turn are at the service of God and of one another.

Understanding this variety in creation helps us grasp better the variety of missions, of services, to welcome the multiplicity while knowing that in it, because of sin, there is the potential for discord (the family of Joseph is a sign of such discord). Such discord, however, once reconciled leads the human family to a better and more profound unity than that indistinct, undifferentiated unity which might be expected from the pure calculation of probabilities regarding human salvation. It is a living reality which is developed around the mystery of Jesus Christ the redeemer, the salvation of humankind, of the Church, of that people of Israel which is the first fruits of Jesus and of the Church. It thus directs humanity in a varied and mobile manner on a journey of salvation which tends toward the heavenly Jerusalem, toward the fullness of God.

You are instruments of this fullness and my wish is that you may be able to grasp the providential nature of your journey in the Church and in the world.

Jesus the Messiah, Son of God and Son of Man

(Homily on the Twenty-sixth Sunday of Ordinary Time)

The Gospel Passage

"John said to him, 'Teacher, we saw someone casting out demons in your name, and we tried to stop him, because he was not following us.' But Jesus said, 'Do not stop him; for no one who does a deed of power in my name will be able soon afterward to speak evil of me. Whoever is not against us is for us. For truly I tell you, whoever gives you a cup of water to drink because you bear the name of Christ will by no means lose the reward. If anyone of you put a stumbling block before one of these little ones who believe in me, it would be better for you if a great millstone were hung around your neck and you were thrown into the sea. If your hand causes you to stumble, cut it off; it is better for you to enter life maimed than to have two hands and to go to hell, to the unquenchable fire. And if your foot causes you to stumble, cut it off; it is better for you to enter life lame than to have two feet and to be thrown into hell. And if your eye causes you to stumble, tear it out; it is better for you to enter the kingdom of God with one eye than to have two eyes and to be thrown into hell, where their worm never dies, and the fire is never quenched" (Mk 9:38-48).

In chapter 8 of the Gospel according to Mark, Jesus has been acknowledged—by Peter, but in the name of the Twelve—as the Christ, the Messiah: "You are the Messiah" (v. 29). At the beginning of chapter 9, in the episode of the Transfiguration, he was revealed as Son: "This is my Son, the Beloved" (v. 7). At the same time, however, Jesus declared himself to be the Son of Man who must suffer much and be despised (cf v. 12).

Mark is thus having us make a progressive journey so that we might better understand the heart of him who is the Messiah of humanity, the Son of the Father, the Son of Man.

In this light we can read the passage of today's liturgy which records some sayings of Jesus. First of all, Jesus takes a position with regard to an assertion by John: we have forbidden a person to cast out demons in your name because *he was not one of ours.* John was convinced of having done the right thing (how many times in the Church's history have his words been repeated: he is ours, he is not ours), but Jesus, the Beloved Son of the Father, tells him that he has erred.

This begins a series of sayings of Jesus. First of all, a general principle: "No one who does a deed of power in my name will be able soon afterward to speak evil of me." The Spirit is one, and whoever says in the Spirit, "Jesus is Lord," cannot then blaspheme him.

"Whoever is not against us is for us": splendid words which express a great interpretative breadth of history and which Jesus applies to the act of charity: "Whoever gives you a cup of water to drink because you bear the name of Christ will by no means lose the reward." The Spirit can move persons in any part of the world to gestures of love.

This promise is followed by the grave threat: "If any of you put a stumbling block before one of these little ones who believe in me, it would be better for you if a great millstone were hung around your neck and you were thrown into the sea." Just as blessed is the one who helps, loves and saves, so woe to those who do evil, and woe to you if you do evil to yourself.

This is a series of words of Jesus which enable us to penetrate his heart, the heart of the Messiah, the Son of the Father, the Son of Man.

I do not want to comment on individual verses but to draw some general reflections, to understand what it means to say that God became human in Jesus and in him makes us his children.

An Important Criterion for Discernment

We have seen, John says, "someone casting out demons." Exorcism is a very important activity in the life of Jesus; while reading Job, we have already meditated on the reality of Satan. Satan is the one who puts evil on the earth, who instills suspicion, who actually tries to make God suspicious of human persons and of their selflessness. Satan is the one who sows discord among individuals, in families, in groups, who leads persons to mutual distrust and envy. He makes the patient expressions of Job unbearable to Job's wife; causes misunderstanding between Anna and Tobit over the goat; and sows jealousy between Joseph and his brothers.

To cast out the demon is to carry out the opposite work. In place of hostility, we sow understanding, in place of envy, altruism, in place of violence, peace, in place of egoism, openness. Whoever accomplishes this work can do so only in the name of Jesus.

What can we derive for ourselves from all this?

A formidable criterion for discernment. Where there are misunderstandings, bitterness, resentment, malice, gossip, there is Satan. Where, instead, we find paths of acceptance, benevolence, respect, mutual esteem, understanding, wherever they come from and whatever label they bear, they are the work of Christ.

Even in places where Jesus is little known, never named, even opposed, we can find acts of patience, of goodness, of charity, brought about by the grace of Christ through the Holy Spirit.

But at the same time we are called to be attentive to whatever is not in this line, no matter what its label, no matter what ideological mode it wears.

We could thus affirm that, making himself human, God dwells in truly human realities, in the sense mentioned above; that he is present wherever there is no opposition to love among persons, even in the smallest actions.

At the same time, God is an inexorable judge of whatever goes against the building up of humanity, of whatever gives scandal, divides, offends, hinders the journey, takes away faith, hope, charity, trust in the future.

This is a vision of Christ the Messiah which on the one hand is very broad, capable of penetrating beyond the visible boundaries of religious confessions. On the other hand, however, it is extremely demanding, capable of judging any action—even if done under the name of Christian—which divides and does not increase love, whether outside of us or within us. Hatred, rancor, and bitterness can bring about the destruction of God's work; we must, therefore, be rigorous judges of ourselves.

Witness to the Humanity of God in Daily Life

In the passage of Mark, therefore, we touch a spark of the mystery of a God who assumed human nature that human nature might be divinized. It is a mystery that extends to the whole of human reality and finds its standard of comparison in the person, in the gestures, in the charitable, constructive, liberating actions of Jesus.

You are constantly inspired by this criterion, to which every action of ours in the Church must conform, in your history as *Equipe Notre Dame,* aided by the great love you have for prayer.

And I believe that love for silent, prolonged prayer is an important sign, which I ask you not to give up, in the certainty that through prayer many apparently impossible situations will find a solution, thanks to the power of God. In this way you proclaim and honor Jesus the Messiah, Son of God and Son of Man. In contemplating his face you draw courage for your activity which wants to make the humanity of God present in the lives of couples and of the human family.

I am certain that this activity is most directly in opposition to contemporary atheism and indifference which, in general, are not due to ideological or theoretical prejudices, as in the last century, but to the struggle persons have to make to see God in daily life, and therefore to the sorrowful sense of the absence of God.

You who feel God present in the small realities of every day life—in the eye, in the hand, in the foot, in the cup of water, in the good word—give the most incisive response to the anguished question of humanity: Where is your God?

Let us therefore ask the Lord that in this Eucharist he may penetrate you, may permeate your marriage promises, so that you may be always better witnesses, in your daily lives, to Jesus the Messiah, Son of God and Son of Man, crucified and risen, witnesses to a God who is near and who is the friend of humanity.

St. Paul Book & Media Centers

ALASKA
750 West 5th Ave., Anchorage, AK 99501; 907-272-8183
CALIFORNIA
3908 Sepulveda Blvd., Culver City, CA 90230; 310-397-8676
5945 Balboa Ave., San Diego, CA 92111; 619-565-9181
46 Geary Street, San Francisco, CA 94108; 415-781-5180
FLORIDA
145 S.W. 107th Ave., Miami, FL 33174; 305-559-6715
HAWAII
1143 Bishop Street, Honolulu, HI 96813; 808-521-2731
ILLINOIS
172 North Michigan Ave., Chicago, IL 60601; 312-346-4228
LOUISIANA
4403 Veterans Memorial Blvd., Metairie, LA 70006; 504-887-7631
MASSACHUSETTS
50 St. Paul's Ave., Jamaica Plain, Boston, MA 02130; 617-522-8911
Rte. 1, 885 Providence Hwy., Dedham, MA 02026; 617-326-5385
MISSOURI
9804 Watson Rd., St. Louis, MO 63126; 314-965-3512
NEW JERSEY
561 U.S. Route 1, Wick Plaza, Edison, NJ 08817; 908-572-1200
NEW YORK
150 East 52nd Street, New York, NY 10022; 212-754-1110
78 Fort Place, Staten Island, NY 10301; 718-447-5071
OHIO
2105 Ontario Street (at Prospect Ave.), Cleveland, OH 44115;
216-621-9427
PENNSYLVANIA
214 W. DeKalb Pike, King of Prussia, PA 19406; 215-337-1882
SOUTH CAROLINA
243 King Street, Charleston, SC 29401; 803-577-0175
TEXAS
114 Main Plaza, San Antonio, TX 78205; 210-224-8101
VIRGINIA
1025 King Street, Alexandria, VA 22314; 703-549-3806
GUAM
285 Farenholt Avenue, Suite 308, Tamuning, Guam 96911;
671-649-4377
CANADA
3022 Dufferin Street, Toronto, Ontario, Canada M6B 3T5;
416-781-9131; 1-800-668-2078